About this book This account of Mackintosh's essential *oeuvre* as a
'poetics of workmanship' shifts the emphasis in Mackintosh
studies from the descriptive to the interpretative. The challenge
Mackintosh set himself was to create a unifying form of modernism for his buildings, interiors and furnishings that took full
account of, among other things, vernacular style and erotic
subjectivity; by concentrating on the decorative aspects of
Mackintosh's originality as an architect and designer, and by
opening up Glasgow's turn of the century world to include, for
example, shipbuilding, art education, Symbolism, the neo-
occult and nascent feminism, the author locates Mackintosh
at the nexus of an unusually rich diversity of influences, all of
which to one degree or another contributed to this architect-
designer's innovatory approach to the arts.

About the author David Brett is currently Reader in the History of
Design at the University of Ulster, Belfast. A former Playwright
in Residence at the Nottingham Playhouse (1963) whose plays
have been translated into German, he is also a novelist (*Black
Folder*, 1976), travel writer (*High Level: The Alps from End to End*, 1983)
and keen mountaineer. He has published numerous articles on
design and related topics, and presently serves on the editorial
board of the art magazine *Circa*. Dr Brett's forthcoming book, *On
Decoration*, will be published in 1992.

C. R. Mackintosh

The Poetics of Workmanship

David Brett

REAKTION BOOKS

Published by Reaktion Books Ltd
79 Farringdon Road
London EC1M 3JU, UK

www.reaktionbooks.co.uk

First published 1992, reprinted 2000

Designed by Humphrey Stone
Photoset by Rowland Photosetting Ltd,
Bury St Edmunds, Suffolk
Colour printed by Balding & Mansell Ltd, Norwich
Printed and bound in Great Britain by
Redwood Books Ltd, Trowbridge, Wiltshire

British Library Cataloguing in Publication Data

Brett, David
Charles Rennie Mackintosh: the poetics of
workmanship.
I. Title
709.2

ISBN 0-948462-23-X
ISBN 0-948462-22-1 (paperback)

Contents

Acknowledgements

Books on scholarly topics now seem, by convention, to require many pages of acknowledgement. This is a practice that ought to be resisted. But I must briefly record my thanks to former colleagues Patrick Eyres and Raymond Buck, with whom I first discussed CRM; to Barbara Freeman, who helped me greatly with illustrations and comments; and to the librarians and my colleagues and students at the University of Ulster. I must also record my thanks to the staffs of the Hunterian Art Gallery, the University of Glasgow Business Archive, the Glasgow Transport Museum, the People's Palace, and others – all of whom gave me their time and good advice.

It goes without saying that I am indebted to numerous other writers, many of whom are not referred to directly. As I was completing the manuscript of this book, new material was being published. Some I have incorporated. William Eadie's *Movements of Modernity: The Case of Glasgow and Art Nouveau* (London 1990) is full of fact and argument relevant to what follows, but it is very different in character and intention. This present book has its origins in an article written for the *Journal of Decorative and Propaganda Arts* in 1988, and in my doctoral thesis (Royal College of Art, London, 1984).

Introduction

The work of the Glasgow architect and designer Charles Rennie Mackintosh (1868–1928) has been often described and extensively studied, but it has usually been interpreted from well within the categories of architectural history and criticism. This short book, however, takes the study of decoration as its starting point, with the intention of enriching our understanding of both buildings and interiors by introducing another perspective.

Mackintosh's career as an architect was relatively short: all his major commissions fall between 1896 and 1906, and these include two institutional buildings in Glasgow – the School of Art (begun in 1897), and Scotland Street School (1904–6) – a small number of private houses (notably Hill House, Helensburgh, of 1902–4), a church, commercial buildings and a series of interiors for various clients. Although a chronological outline of Mackintosh's life and work is appended (see pages 146–9) it will be useful, none the less, to think of his career in the following six stages:

Apprenticeship As a draughtsman to well-established Glaswegian architects, and as a student at the Glasgow School of Art (1884–92).

Early work The junior member of a partnership, designing interiors and details of buildings, and gaining a growing reputation as part-creator of the Glasgow Style, a northern Art Nouveau.

Acclaim Following the design of the new Glasgow School of Art (1896) and several other commissions he becomes an equal partner in his firm, and (with his wife, Margaret Macdonald) gains an international reputation as an original decorative designer and architect.

1 Charles Rennie Mackintosh with Hamish R. Davidson, 1898.

Decline Fame abroad is not matched by commissions at home. Depression and lack of work lead to resignation from his firm and departure for England in 1914.

Late style Begins to re-establish his career in London, as a designer of textiles and interiors. Architectural projects come to nothing.

Last years Throws up what few opportunities he had developed and devotes himself to painting from 1923 until his death in 1928.

In terms of quantity, the career outlined above was that of an original but only moderately successful provincial architect, one who overreached himself and fell on hard times. In terms of quality, however, the Mackintosh *oeuvre* has always been regarded as exceptional. It is not difficult to see why this should be so. Each of the designs and completed buildings exhibits a unity of style and feeling that commands attention: both large and small features seem to grow through every detail of his buildings, down to carpets, furniture, light-fittings, wallpapers, weather-vanes and even cutlery. The ambition to do this was present in many of his contemporaries, but none achieved it to such a degree and with such finesse. It is not necessary to like the designs to feel the presence of this organizing power. Indeed, the all-encompassing quality of a Mackintosh interior, in which spaces and surfaces all lead into one another and are integrated into the very structure of the building, can be an unnerving experience; it is hard to resist becoming acutely self-conscious. But the power is undeniable. At the same time, the buildings have proved to be practical: the School of Art (which has been long considered as one of the finest educational buildings of the past century) has been maintained virtually unaltered and with little repair for several generations of students.

If Mackintosh's career as a successful architect was short, his parallel work as a designer of interiors, furniture and most forms of decorative art was long. When his architectural life went into decline, out of it he developed a new approach to decoration; and when this second career failed to flower he took to painting with great seriousness. Indeed, had none of his other lives been lived so thoroughly, he might now be remembered as a noteworthy watercolourist and botanical illustrator.

Mackintosh worked at the centre of a group of designers and decorative artists who created what came to be known as the Glasgow Style. This style was a northern Art Nouveau, and there are many points of similarity between the graphic, textile, furniture and other work produced by the Scots and that by their contemporaries in Paris, Brussels, Darmstadt, Vienna and other European cities. (And there were personal and commercial, as well as stylistic, connections.) The Glasgow Style was far more admired in Budapest and Turin than ever it was in London; nor is it fortuitous that the Glasgow Style can be compared to work that was being produced at the same time in Chicago and New York. What all these creative projects shared was the search for modernity; they were part of a much wider quest for forms of life and art that would express the sense of entering into a new epoch. This required the bringing together of a scientific understanding of the world with a subjective and intuitive spirit, and it was to be expressed through an all-embracing style that owed little or nothing to the past. Like Art Nouveau and the Jugendstil, the Glasgow Style did not survive beyond the first decade of this century, but it evolved from an elaborate biomorphic imagery towards a geometrical and tectonic manner that has been seen as an early form of 'Modernism'.

Architects and writers upon architecture have always seen Mackintosh as an important designer, but for a number of distinct and, indeed, incompatible reasons. His European contemporaries saw him and the other members of the Glasgow Style as the most advanced aesthetes of their day. Hermann Muthesius in his seminal book, *Das englische Haus* (1904–5), described the 'white interiors' that Mackintosh and his wife designed for themselves and for a few other clients as 'refined to a degree which the lives of even the artistically educated are still a long way from matching . . . they are the milestones placed by a genius far ahead of us to mark the way to excellence for mankind in the future'.[1] Another commentator wrote of 'the lyrical sublimation of the practical . . . here were rooms like dreams'.[2] The potent influence of Mackintosh and of Margaret Macdonald on Central European taste is now well recognized. But English critics of the time were less rhapsodic, and spoke of a 'spook school' of 'unhealthy' tendencies. In the former case, the favourable reception abroad was given to the decorative aspects of their work; the architectural being largely known through published drawings, rather than through acquaintance with actual buildings. In the latter case, as I argue below, the English rejection of

Scots modernity was part of a more general cultural timidity.

A later group of critics, writing between the two World Wars, saw Mackintosh through the spectacles of polemical 'Modernism'; for them, the decorative aspect of his architecture was unacceptable, and was even attributed to the baleful influence of his wife. It is a striking fact that the Viennese in 1900 regarded the two as equal collaborators, whereas in 1933 P. Morton Shand – an influential writer on modern design – urged the organizers of a Mackintosh memorial exhibition that 'the exhibition may not be so arranged as to give the impression that Mrs Mackintosh was in any sense considered her husband's equal or alter ego'.[3] From the perspective of the International Style, it was reasonable to see the constructive and functional aspects of Mackintosh's architecture as a precursor of the Modern Movement. This is an attitude that was to strongly influence Mackintosh's first biographer, Thomas Howarth, and that persuasive scholar Nikolaus Pevsner. But as Robert Macleod wrote in 1968, this interpretation sits 'very uneasily in any campaign which numbered among its goals the rejection of tradition, the glorification of new technology, the rejection of ornament, and the substitution of cool generalization for intense individuality. If he intended to be modern, it was never in that way'.[4]

Macleod and other recent writers have been at pains to stress Mackintosh's inheritance, doing their best to locate him more firmly in the context of the Arts and Crafts Movement, and in the 'free-style' architecture of late nineteenth-century Britain. Macleod has gone so far as to describe him as 'a last and remote efflorescence of a vital British tradition which reached back to Pugin . . . one of the last and one of the greatest Victorians'.[5] Others have connected Mackintosh's work to the contemporary interest in Japanese models that was especially prevalent in Glasgow during the years of his apprenticeship, and to concerns that were specifically Scottish, stressing the regional character of the buildings. This more recent tendency is part of the wider and welcome re-evaluation of nineteenth-century architecture and design; and there is no doubt that this has added more to our understanding than the openly polemic approach of the Modernists. At a time when it is not clear just what a modern architecture could or might be, the relationships now discerned between his past and the future are illuminating.

Most recently of all, the phenomenon of the Glasgow Style itself has received much attention, with attempts being made to see Mackintosh as the first among equals rather than as a solitary genius. This has led, in particular, to a reassessment of Margaret Macdonald and her sister Frances, and of other designers of the period. The highly evolved cultural life of Glasgow (or part of it, at least) has come in for some detailed study, and has been the subject of exhibitions and publications connected with Glasgow's year in 1990 as Europe's 'City of Culture'.

The character of the city of Glasgow is of some importance in any interpretation of Mackintosh's life and work; during his early life it became the second city of the largest political empire that has ever existed, supplying up to half the world's ocean-going ships and a large proportion of its railway engines and carriages. Glasgow was also the centre of a large textiles industry. The city stood in relation to north-west Europe as Chicago stands to the Great Plains of North America. It was also notable for technical and scientific education, and, for a brief while, its artistic life was more widespread and ambitious than that of London. Mackintosh was not its only remarkable architect, and the Glasgow School of Art, under the energetic direction of Francis Newbery, was recognized as one of Europe's leading design schools.

If Mackintosh's work is examined exclusively from an architectural standpoint, some aspects of it are difficult to explain. For example, in Glasgow, shipbuilding and other industries had created a demand for immense numbers of skilled craftspeople and technicians. The School of Art, where Mackintosh and most of his later associates studied, was only one of several institutions in which this work-force was to be trained. The School of Art had begun as one of the many Government-sponsored Schools of Design, and its principal function remained that of educating 'industrial artists' and 'ornamentalists'. Its basic curriculum, originally ordained by the British Department of Science and Art, was the so-called 'South Kensington system', which stressed orderly learning and an attention to drawing. Under Newbery's direction, broader, and in some respects antithetical, teachings were introduced. The craft-based and scholarly approach of the Arts and Crafts Movement formed a second aspect of the instruction, and a strongly blended vein of Symbolism and the neo-occult formed a third. None of these tendencies was primarily architectural, and the consequences of this intellectual nexus are explored in the pages that follow.

In addition to these influences there was a robust sense of national identity and the desire, among some architects at least, to render it in built form. Well before international 'Modernism', the nineteenth century had recognized that industrial production was tending to produce the same material conditions everywhere, with a consequent decay in local character. Mackintosh shared this concern just as much as he and his colleagues were seeking a modern form of expression. The question was always the same: How could the two be reconciled? The tension in Mackintosh's work between the objective, containing structure of each building – all of which have strong neo-vernacular elements – and the 'contents', the rooms and fittings, which are invested with a lyrical subjectivity of the most modern kind, has its source in the challenge set by this question. Mackintosh's architecture can be interpreted as an attempt to create what recently has been called a 'critical regionalism', in which modernity of feeling, universal technology and a respect for locality are all held in balance.

That a body of work can bear various and detailed interpretations shows that it is rich and rewarding of study. Mackintosh's work, and that of his wife and other designers of the Glasgow group, occurred at the meeting-place of several forms of discourse, of which the architectural is only one. The discourse of decoration, a most typical nineteenth-century concern, is another, and the relation of local character to universal technology is a third. In this book I offer an interpretation, a 'poetics'; but I wish at the outset to stress that my poetics is one possible interpretation, and not one that makes any claim to completeness. The process of interpretation should be liberating in its effect, opening up the world to our curiosity. Moreover, this book is not a thesis, and therefore a single and exclusive line of thought is not developed; some of my conclusions are speculative and in certain places I have permitted myself to be conjectural. It may be useful, then, to indicate what I do not attempt. Since I concentrate upon the years up to 1909, and on particular interiors, there is no discussion of Mackintosh's interesting late career as a painter, and little about what may be called his Northampton Style, which developed as Mackintosh attempted to rebuild a career for himself in England during the years of the Great War. Nor have I dealt with architecture in strictly architectural terms: there is no extended treatment of the problems of meeting a design brief, for example, nor of methods of construction, nor of the main problems of composition. And, of course, in a short book some complicated matters have to be treated brusquely; among them is the Arts and Crafts Movement, which I have tended to treat as more unified and programmatic than it was in reality. I do, however, attempt to shift Margaret Macdonald more to the centre of events than others have done; this is, in part, because I identify the discourse of femininity as being especially important to our understanding of the Glasgow Style.

I have done my best not to write in a technical manner, hoping throughout that the interested reader will find this book pleasurable; where there is no pleasure there is neither learning nor art, and to write a book that was ugly or obscure about buildings and designs that are neither would be repugnant. Like many others who have studied their work, I have developed a tenderness for C. R. and M. Mackintosh; if this book carried a dedication, it would be to their breathless shades.

1 The City and the Context

We begin with the city. To do so is not to imply that the work of Mackintosh and his associates was, in some simple sense, wholly determined by its 'context'; nor is it to argue that we have to understand the context before we can interpret the work. Still less does it 'explain' either the work or the man. Relations between the individual and the social cannot be reduced to 'determination', though they include determinants; and the interpretation of any work of the past is, simultaneously, the creation of a context through which the work is given meaning. The description of Mackintosh's 'context' below forms part of the interpretation that follows.

The realm of the young Mackintosh was not simply that of architecture; it also included artists' studios, the world of the shipyards in which so many of his colleagues were employed, and education, for his studies and apprenticeship were conducted at a time when the haphazard but practical methods of one century were being replaced by the professionalization of another. Mackintosh's strictly practical architectural training was in the older mode, but he spent a large slice of his life – both as a student and as a practitioner – attached to one of Europe's most advanced art and design colleges. The sum of these intersecting domains was a very rich practical and intellectual working environment.

The civic culture of Glasgow in the latter half of the nineteenth century deserves close study. Glasgow, which straddles the River Clyde, was strategically placed between Europe and America; its hinterland was rich in minerals and coal, and its population well-educated. Glasgow was, in fact, perfectly poised to become what, in 1905, an American visitor was to describe as 'the most aggressively efficient city in Great Britain'. Well before this, the architectural profession had identified it as a city to be watched: in *The Builder* (14 April 1855) it was reported that, so far as modern technology was concerned, 'Glasgow . . . is at the present time the most go-ahead city in Great Britain'. It was popularly known as 'the second city of the Empire'. The impression of its energy was increased by the very crowded character of Glasgow's centre. A number of geographers have remarked on this, describing it as a city turned inside out; one that acted as a dormitory to its industrial satellites:

> Glasgow never developed symptoms of suburban sprawl typical of many other cities until well into the twentieth century, and remains an extraordinarily compact and densely populated city. . . . You took from your populous centre workmen to work away from the centre and you brought them back at night . . . as the city increased, the works were sent out into the countryside and the population remained.[6]

The works were textiles, locomotive construction and, above all, the vast shipbuilding and shipfitting industries on the Clyde. Each in their turn fed upon and helped to generate an enormous infrastructure and numerous ancillary trades, not the least of which were in the decorative arts. The region's artistic activities were as much engaged in these industries as they were in its architecture.

The scale of Glasgow's shipbuilding was phenomenal; most authorities reckon that in 1900 – when Mackintosh's career was entering its most fruitful years – up to half the existing world tonnage, mercantile and naval, had been built on Clydeside. To understand and interpret the working environment of Mackintosh and his contemporaries, it is important first to have some grasp of the size and scope of Glasgow's fitting-out trades. The reason for this is that, although Mackintosh himself seems never to have been involved in any of them, nearly all his contemporaries and colleagues were – as designers, draughtsmen or consultants; and nearly all the firms for which Mackintosh made designs, and which he used as contractors on his own commissions, spent as much, if not more, of their time working for shipyards than for architects. The professional and trade context of the decorative arts on Glasgow was not one of patient craftsmanship, but of high-speed, technically advanced, semi-industrial production. In this respect, the Glasgow Style was like contemporaneous manifestations of Art Nouveau elsewhere in Europe, linked to the highest levels of capitalism, to modern transport, electricity and the most sophisticated methods of production. The Glasgow School of Art was founded for the purpose of providing these trades with a stream of trained young people, but during Mackintosh's time in the School the emphasis changed from these utilitarian and commercial ends towards an educational ethos that was increasingly art and craft oriented. The mis-match between the real working world of Mackintosh's maturity and the expectations he had of it is a factor that has a bearing on the trajectory of his career.

There is no human activity that requires so many skills, sciences, trades, crafts and arts as the designing, building and fitting out of large vessels. The implications of this for the decorative artists and craftworkers of Glasgow were extensive; the years from 1895 to 1910 were those of the greatest activity in luxury shipbuilding that the world has ever seen. These were the years in which the transatlantic and oriental lines went from being the conveyors of mass emigration in cheap discomfort to being providers of carefully structured hierarchies of comfort and style to different classes of passenger. The interior design of the liners built for this new market expressed social differentiation on a scale that extended from basic efficiency to elaborate splendour. What accompanied this was a new effectiveness in many services, such as plumbing, air-conditioning, heating and electric lighting.

It is important to recognize these facts, for Mackintosh's context has been described as the 'tight, little professional world of Glasgow architects'.[7] But this 'tight little' architectural domain overlapped and interacted with the shipfitting world at several points, through a number of firms and individuals. For once the hull of a ship had been launched, it was the custom to hand over the design of its cabins and state-rooms, and the details of the superstructure, to an architect and his posse of contractors.

The precise points of interaction between architecture and shipfitting are difficult to locate because the ships themselves have long since gone down to the fishes or been sent to the breakers' yards; moreover, there has been a wholesale destruction of the records of the relevant yards. There are, however, some matters about which we can be quite certain, one of which is the collaboration between Halsey Ricardo (1854–1928) and William De Morgan (1839–1917). Ricardo was a London-based architect whose decorative interiors are particularly fine; his style was highly individual and

2 Saloon on the SS
Arabia (launched
1898) designed by
Halsey Ricardo
with William De
Morgan.

3 Saloon on the
Fürst Bismarck
(launched 1905).

Built at Fairfield's
Yard, the Fürst
Bismarck had
unusually restrained
interior decoration.
Whoever designed
these chairs seems to
have been familiar
with the Glasgow
Style, then at its
height. Since one of
the firms listed in the
contract book (for
carpeting and
upholstery) is Wylie &
Lochead, it is possible
that the designer of
this saloon and its
fittings was E. A.
Taylor. The main part
of these elegant chairs
have evidently been
fitted onto the
cast-iron supports of
an earlier design.

tended toward a severe Art Nouveau manner. In *The Archi-tecture of Glasgow* (1968), Gomme and Walker mention Ricardo as a possible influence on the young Mackintosh, apparently without knowing of Ricardo's many Glaswegian commissions, though it is probable that he did not advertise this work since it was regarded as a good deal less pres-tigious than 'real' building. De Morgan, famous for his lustrous tile-work and the leading ceramicist of the Aes-thetic Movement, already had some important experience of shipfitting: between 1889 and 1900 he and Ricardo collab-orated on the interiors of a series of liners for the Peninsular and Oriental Steamship Company, which were built in the yards of Caird, of Stephens and of Fairfield. The two men were responsible for the decor of the *China* (1889), the *Malta*, *Palawan* and *Sumatra* (1895), the *Arabia* (1898; illus. 2) and the *Persia* (1900) – vessels that gave their first-class passengers the experience of a floating Aesthetic Movement. Today, scarcely a trace of this work remains.[8]

The years of this collaboration are the years in which Mack-intosh, starting as a junior draughtsman in the firm of Honey-man & Keppie, established himself as a designer of great promise. His speciality within the partnership was the com-pletion of interiors, of which the Glasgow Art Club (in 1893) was the most wholly his own. There is every reason to assume that the contractors with whom he would have worked would also have been working, simultaneously, on shipfitting con-tracts. Such contracts, with their very precise deadlines, pre-fabrication and systems of 'putting out' work, required a very different approach to draughtsmanship, management and quality control than did the more traditional organization of a normal building contract. Whatever Mackintosh's aspirations were in terms of perfect cooperation between architect, crafts-man and artist, they were hardly to be realized in such con-ditions. Aspects of his later style, especially where woodwork is concerned, suggest a designer impatient of on-site con-struction and one who was determined to express the 'assembled' nature of his work.

Another architect who worked on shipfitting commissions was William Leiper; he employed De Morgan on the interiors of the *Livadia*, a yacht built specially for the Tsar of Russia. Launched in 1880, the *Livadia* was a remarkable craft in many respects, not least for the immense luxury of its fittings. The reception rooms of this floating palace were in the style of Louis XVI, the drawing-rooms in 'Crimean-Tartar', and the private rooms 'in the simple kind of modern English, regard being made for the greatest comfort'.[9] There was also Andrew Wells, a partner in the firm of Guthrie & Wells, which specialized in glass, furniture and interior design. Guthrie & Wells commissioned designs from a number of Glaswegian artists, including the young Mackintosh, and, in turn, they were later employed as contractors on several Mackintosh commissions.

While the P. & O. Line dominated the eastern sea-routes, Cunard was struggling to wrest transatlantic supremacy from their two rivals, White Star and Inman, by commissioning yet more expensive vessels. The *Campania* and *Lucania*, built by John Brown in 1893, set new standards of opulence. For these vessels Cunard employed James Miller, the Glasgow architect who was soon to be responsible for the overall design of the Glasgow Exhibition of 1901. Miller was also a designer and consultant to the firm of Wylie & Lochead, whose very large furniture and interiors business was one of the main outlets of the Glasgow Style. Miller does not appear to have brought the new style into his liners, but he certainly employed Glasgow artists for particular details. His interiors and fittings for the *Lusitania* (1907) included stained glass by Oscar Patterson and enamelled panels by Alexander Fisher. Since Miller knew Mackintosh and his friends, and since Mackintosh had designed not only part of the 1901 exhibition but also projects for its concert hall, one cannot help wondering whether a floating 'white interior' or a transatlantic tea-room once existed. . . . The nearest we can come to this fancy is with the interiors of the *Fürst Bismarck*, built at Fairfield's Yard for the Hamburg-Amerika Line and launched in 1905. Photographs suggest that the unknown designer of its interiors was acquainted with the Glasgow Style and with similar movements in Germany and Austria. It is striking how modern these rooms and cabins look when compared with the clumsy eclecticism of Miller's work for Cunard (illus. 3).[10] The fixtures and fittings were done on Clydebank by Hoskins & Sons and by the ubiquitous Wylie & Lochead who, in the same year, were selling 'art furniture' designed by Mackintosh's colleagues at their store in Buchanan Street.

Wylie & Lochead advertised themselves as 'Specialists in

fitting of steamships and yachts, complete furnishings of hotels, clubs, shooting lodges and bungalows.' Thus the same, or similar, products appeared interchangeably for land or sea. The firm was a great employer of freelance and sub-contracting craftsmen; by examining such records as remain, one gains the impression that both it and Guthrie & Wells, and other concerns too, carved up the available contracts according to convenience – passing jobs backwards, forwards and sideways among Glasgow's numerous workshops and craftspeople. Furnishings and decor originally designed for ships were frequently to be found in hotels and mansions and, of course, vice versa. These promiscuous design practices were what Mackintosh, with his passion for unity, was concerned to avoid; but they were a part of his working environment, and he had to fit in with them or find his own way.

Michael Donnelly, in a still unfinished labour of research, has identified a whole series of small firms that worked together and in competition with one another between 1880 and 1910, servicing both the building industry and the profitable ship construction that largely financed Glasgow's architecture. He makes the important point that 'at a time when the Ruskin–Morris ideal of the artist-craftsman was achieving universal ascendancy, they were to establish a reputation on the basis of employing freelance designers, few of whom were craftsmen'.[11] This observation should modify the view that Mackintosh and his colleagues adhered directly to the values of the Arts and Crafts Movement, since their actual practice was in this respect at variance with their recorded words.

In a lecture, often quoted, entitled 'Architecture' (1893), Mackintosh insisted that to get 'true architecture the architect must be one of a body of artists possessing an intimate knowledge of the crafts. . . . There must be a real communion and a working together. . .'.[12] Had Mackintosh been able to work in such a community he might have avoided the frequent accusation that his furniture and detailing was flimsy and impractical. Under such circumstances, quality control was a difficult and pressing problem. At the same time, the existence of a semi-industrial environment held out the real possibility of uniting individually designed high quality with large-batch production, thus enabling an artistic intervention into the everyday. Overall, the Glasgow Style should be viewed as much from this perspective as from a more conventional history of styles. It appears, commercially, as just one among many available styles that could be supplied 'from stock' and applied in whatever circumstances a client might demand. Thus, although the Glasgow Style was in principle predicated on a programme of social and spiritual reform, it was, because of the circumstances of its production and distribution, immediately available as yet another commodity. The avant-garde aspects of the Style are tied in with its commercial possibilites.

We should further note that though these numerous firms were small, they had international ramifications, which helped to spread Glasgow's decorative arts around the world. Daniel Cottier's studio, in particular, grew to establish branches in Australia and the United States, while Guthrie & Wells commissioned the painter David Gauld to design windows in Buenos Aires. The designs and workmanship of these firms were on constant display to almost every sea-borne traveller, and in Continental Europe reached as far as Moscow. It is also worth remarking here that there was a strong Scots component in the English Aesthetic Movement, well before the emergence of the distinct Glasgow Style. In addition to Cottier (who was very well known in London) there were designers such as J. Moyr Smith (who began as an apprentice to the Glasgow architectural dynasty of the Salmon family) and Bruce J. Talbert, best known for his Aesthetic textiles and furniture. Glasgow-born Christopher Dresser returned to his native city to find a suitable manufacturer for his Clutha glassware, which led him to the firm of James Couper Ltd. This company was responsible for a number of products by Aesthetic Movement designers, as well as for coloured and stained glass of very high quality. Both Walter Crane and C. F. A. Voysey designed carpets for the Glasgow manufacturer James Templeton.

We should also note the possible contribution of ship technology to building practice.[13] Major vessels, particularly those for the oriental lines, were remarkable for their highly developed services. The services and technology of the Glasgow School of Art, designed by Mackintosh in 1897, have often been praised for their ingenuity and modernity. But ducted heating and ventilation were regarded as so essential in ships that they were routinely fitted. The device of the 'master' clock and its subsidiary 'slaves', ensuring identical timekeeping all over the vessel (or, in this case, School) was already a regular feature on board ships, where they were often fitted by the Glaswegian firm of W. C. Martin. The method whereby the ceiling of the Library of the School of Art is hung from the joists of an upper room, thought to be unusual from the perspective of conventional architecture was, and still is, a common device in ship construction.

The question inevitably arises as to what degree did Mackintosh avail himself of the existing expertise when he designed the School and its services? This is not a question that can easily be answered, since no records survive that could provide us with detailed information. But it is a reasonable inference that, surrounded with an extraordinary concentration of skills, he should have learned from it. There is, moreover, something in the plan of the School of Art, with its central corridor and stairwells, that recalls the deck-plan of a ship (with engine-room below) as much as any college building then in existence. The upper galleries of the School, which look out over the sea of Glasgow's roofs, suggest marine analogies to many visitors. Thirty years after the School was built, Le Corbusier popularized the transatlantic liner as a source for sound design; but it may be that the Scots architect had been there before him. Whatever was the case, here I am mainly concerned with establishing a further dimension to the accepted picture of architectural practice at the turn of the century by pointing out that Mackintosh had available to him in Glasgow one of the greatest concentrations of design technicians and service engineers to be found anywhere in the world. In assessing the 'context' of the Glasgow Style, this should be taken into account, since the several Arts Nouveaux all distinguished themselves from earlier movements by an embrace of what Patrick Geddes (1854–1932), as early as 1898, was calling the 'neotechnic order, characterised by electricity, hygiene and art'.[14]

Just as firms moved back and forth within this busy network, so did individuals. A typical example is E. A. Taylor. As a chief designer for Wylie & Lochead, Taylor was at the centre of the Glasgow Style and was its most industrially experienced proponent. The Larners suggest that he was responsible for the art-furniture of the Company during the crucial years 1901–8, and that his use of interchangeable elements, such as hinges, handles and motifs, helped to ensure a unity of house style. Taylor's interiors shown at the Glasgow Exhibition of 1901 were singled out by Hermann Muthesius for praise in the influential German magazine *Dekorative Kunst*, and his work was a major part of the Glasgow contribution to the Turin Exhibition held the following year. But Taylor began his career as an engineering draughtsman at the foundry of Scott & Co. at nearby Greenock; and he had also taught at the Glasgow and West of Scotland Technical College, which was a centre for the training of draughtsmen and industrial craftworkers of many kinds.[15]

For a clearer picture of the forces at work in Mackintosh's early experiences, we need to assess the educational world in which he and his colleagues grew up. Mackintosh belonged to a new and distinct social formation – those trained to a high level in design. Glasgow's industries had an insatiable demand for the visually competent: every boy with a drawing talent (and some girls too) was likely to find a way into a draughtsman's office. Most of these young people then passed through one of a number of design institutions, to which they were usually sent by their employers as apprentices. Glasgow's Technical College, where Taylor taught, had some claim to being the oldest institution of its type in Europe, having been founded as early as 1796. Among its notable professors were George Birkbeck (who founded the Mechanics' Institutes) and Andrew Ure (whose surveys of manufacturing industry are important source-books for the historian of design and technology). Among its first students was James Watt. During Mackintosh's early years the number of students enrolled rose from 2000 in 1888 to 4600 in 1900; and of the latter number, 344 were in the Department of Industrial Arts and 616 in the Department of Architecture. There they received instruction in the skilled trades and most left with a certificate, though some more able students could take a University of Glasgow degree. By far the greater number of those enrolled were evening-class students, many of whom received grants from the Glasgow Corporation.

The School of Art (founded in 1844) where Mackintosh spent some eight years of his life, contained a further 840 students by 1900, of which many were part-time and evening enrolments. In one contemporary survey it was noted that 'the art of design claims the studies of the majority'.[16] If we add to the students at the School of Art, the further 809 students who attended the art classes run by the School Board, and the 100 who were in the College of Weaving, Dyeing and Printing, we gain a total of at least 2700 students engaged in design-relevant studies at any one time within Glasgow. There were also art (i.e. design) institutes in Paisley and other neighbouring towns. This is a considerable total by any standard, and gives some indication of the importance attached to design and to the decorative trades. It also helps to place Mackintosh within a social formation that maintained a tension between commercial and aesthetic principles, a problematic and highly educated group whose livelihoods were largely dependent upon patterns of investment and consumption over which they had absolutely no control. Glasgow was ripe for an avant-garde.

As I have already noted, by 1900 the School had in fact turned away from its utilitarian origins toward more artistic ends. In doing so, it was entering into that same discontinuous and problematic relationship with light industry and craftsmanship that Mackintosh was experiencing. This is a further element in that context I am constructing, and its importance will be investigated in the next chapter, where I shall show that the curriculum of the School of Art, and the contradictions it contained, is one of the keys to the interpretation of Mackintosh's work.

There is another dimension to the context under discussion: that of the painter's studio. This was a professional and intellectual situation with which Mackintosh had very close links. He was himself an accomplished painter, who in his last years devoted all his time to the art; he was a friend of the leading Glasgow artists of the day (David Gauld gave him one of his first commissions, which was for some bedroom furniture), and Mackintosh's wife, Margaret Macdonald, was a painter and graphic artist of original talent. But most important of all, it was the contemporary concerns of painters that provided Mackintosh with the conceptual framework that enabled him to surpass his architectural training.

The 'Ecole de Glasgow' enacted on a more modest scale a similar trajectory to that of the Ecole de Paris. Beginning in a Realism that was the artistic fruit of early nineteenth-century Positivism, it concluded in Symbolism and a tendency to transcendental emotion that was the dialectical counterweight to its point of origin. In terms of subject-matter, this was a progression from narrative to decoration, from descriptive to formal values. This passage was undoubtedly influenced by the close links that existed between Glasgow and Paris, and between Glasgow and the numerous small colonies of painters in France and Belgium; but it was also a typical feature of nineteenth-century artistic development, which grew from the logical development of its fundamental premises. Such a trajectory could, of course, be interrupted by distractions or timidity, and not all artists moved so far along it as some managed to do.[17] None of the Glasgow artists, it must be said, contemplated the final step into abstraction. We can see the farthest development of Glasgow painting in the work of Edward Hornel, George Henry and David Gauld around 1889–90, and in Hornel's Japanese paintings of 1894. In these canvases a fine line was trodden between decoration and narrative, and between a deep pictorial space and a shallow colour field. As one German critic noted, these works 'approach the border where painting ends and the Persian carpet begins'.[18]

The analogy with the Persian carpet, made either in praise or disparagement, is a typical critical ploy of the latter part of the century. It marks the growing convergence between the fine and the decorative arts; there are numerous examples from all over Europe in which a spiral of mutual interaction between these two spurred more intense and radical activity. In either case, we are concerned with a greater degree of abstraction and with the growing autonomy of pictorial elements and decorative motifs. This principle of convergence has been called the 'carpet paradigm'.[19] By the mid-1880s, for a painting to be likened to a carpet or tapestry was, in Post-Impressionist circles, a singular point of praise. And this textile analogy was always with Persian or other oriental exemplars, which were 'flat' in terms of pictorial space and abstract in design. In time this was to lead to the first non-figurative painting.

The paintings of both Hornel and Henry were steps on this way. The isolation of pure decorative motifs into pictorial elements, which can be seen in *The Druids Bringing Home the Mistletoe* (1890; illus. 20), are comparable to similar strategies invoked by Gauguin or, later, Klimt. The use made of the frame, whereby the gilded torc in the painting is repeated, unifies the picture plane with the real surface, and with the real world, in a manner similar to that employed by Jan Toorop in several contemporaneous works. In paintings such as these, Glasgow's leading artists were on the brink of a fully developed Symbolist movement, one close to those of their Continental peers.

The actual step into that different philosophical world (idealist and quasi-mystical) was taken by a small group of students, mostly female, at the School of Art; this group included Margaret Macdonald and her sister Frances.[20] The graphic vocabulary of this circle was drawn from diverse sources – *The Yellow Book*, illustrations in *The Studio*, the painting of Toorop and Ferdinand Khnopf, and Japanese and Celtic art. The neo-occult imagery that occurs in their work is directly comparable to that adopted by French, Belgian and Dutch contemporaries. The Glasgow Style was set in motion by these young people, who gave it its peculiar character – metamorphic, eroticized and dreamy. Mackintosh came into the circle at a time when this graphic vocabulary was already partly formed, and his assimilation of its character was enmeshed in his profound attachment to Margaret Macdonald. I argue later that the eroticized idealism running all through Mackintosh's early work, and which is in tension with the empiricist and 'common sense' values of the Arts and Crafts Movement (which he also espoused), is the key to understanding his architecture. It is expressed in the interior designs in particular, in the rooms that were conceived as artistic compositions of equal status and character to Symbolist paintings. These were not values and attitudes that could be gained within the world of Glasgow's architects; but they were factors that greatly assisted the rising reputation of the Glasgow Style in Continental Europe, from 1895 onward.

In gaining a reputation abroad above that which it gained at home, the Glasgow Style (and Mackintosh and Macdonald in particular) was following a path already smoothed for it by Glasgow's painters. The connections between Glasgow and Continental centres were firm and numerous, with interchange either way. This culminated in the invitation of the Glasgow Boys to exhibit with the Munich Secession in 1893. The easy internationalism of Glasgow's studios is another element in Mackintosh's mental world that was not gained in his architectural training.

The importance of the Symbolist connection is illustrated by the appointment to the School of Art of Jean Delville (1867–1953), who was employed as its professor of painting from 1901 to 1906 (though his attendance may not have been continuous). Delville was also a writer and a theorist, with a long-standing interest in theosophy and spiritualism. As an exhibitor at the Rose & Croix Salon he was a direct link with the world of 'Sar' Peladan and Les Nabis, and thus with Gustave Moreau, Odilon Redon and Gauguin. He was a leading proponent of the artistic aspects of theosophy and well known in Dutch circles, in which members of the Theosophical Society mingled with painters such as Piet Mondrian and architects such as J. L. M. Lauweriks and Karel de Bazel. When Delville left Glasgow in 1906 he was replaced by another Belgian teacher.

So far, I have attempted to place the young Mackintosh at the meeting place of three worlds – of the decorative arts and trades in the context of shipfitting, of an educational system, and of an artistic milieu with international connections. But before attempting to assess what might be made from this, and before moving onto the central ground of architecture, we should also take note of the fact that within the strictly intellectual realm, the University of Glasgow was the fountainhead of Associationism, an aesthetic philosophy that guided all nineteenth-century architectural criticism.

We need not assume that Mackintosh had read the classic texts of Associationist aesthetics: there is no evidence he was widely read beyond the immediate concerns of his practice. Nor was it necessary that he should have done, since the broad assumptions of the School of so-called Scottish Common Sense philosophy were common currency. Francis Hutcheson, who may be taken to be the father of the School, held the chair of Moral Philosophy in Glasgow University from 1729 until his death in 1747. Hutcheson's ideas were taken up and linked with David Hume's philosophy by Dugald Stewart and Thomas Reid (the latter held the chair between 1763 and 1781), and by Adam Smith. But they enter most directly into writings on art in Archibald Alison's *Essays on the Nature and Principles of Taste* (1790), a book that was widely available, often reprinted and frequently paraphrased.[21] Alison's key assumption, largely developed from earlier writers, was that Beauty did not inhere in objects themselves, but existed only in the mind of the beholder. Perception of what was thought to be Beautiful depended on the mind's capacity to make complex series of 'associations', which in turn could be recalled in ever-modified forms by the act of 'imagination'. The ability to evoke such associations in the mind was explained as the power of 'expression'. Where architecture was concerned, all depended upon understanding the true function of a building: if the associations it generated in the mind of the beholder did not fit with its actual function, then it was not well designed. Numerous writers have seen in this relationship between function and association the origins of modern 'functionalist' concepts of beauty.[22] But it also paved the way for eclecticism, revivalism and the modern concept of 'styling'.

Associationist ideas were the very marrow of Victorian architectural criticism and one aspect of this in particular is worth special mention – the tendency that was then current to see architectural forms and aspects of design in terms of gender. A style or a feature would often be described as 'masculine' or 'feminine', and sometimes as 'effeminate'.[23] Construction was regarded as a masculine domain, decoration as feminine. Frequently allied to this were organic analogies; and it is clear that these did not simply remain as figures of speech but served as guides to practice. Gender associations were both read into and reproduced in architectural form and ornament, and this can be traced throughout Mackintosh's architecture and interior design. His buildings, from the details of their interior decoration to their outward masses and volumes, were designed with a keen eye on their evoking the proper associations. The relationships between these directed responses and the means by which they are evoked form a system that I describe in Chapter 3 as a 'poetics'.

We know, in fact, that Mackintosh was strongly opposed to anti-Associationist aesthetics, since he was a keen reader of W. H. Lethaby's writings, in which the symbolic associations of architecture were shown to carry the essential meaning. Moreover, we find in Mackintosh's own lecture on 'Seemliness' that among the 'props of art' is 'the absurd and false idea – that there can be any living emotion expressed in work scientifically proportioned according to ancient principles'.[24] During Mackintosh's early life, the Common Sense School came under criticism from a renewed Idealist and Hegelian philosophy, represented in the writings of Bernard Bosanquet and Edward Caird. It seems to me unlikely that Mackintosh was acquainted with these directly, but they may well have contributed toward the more general climate of Idealism that accompanied the rise of the Glasgow Style. Such Idealism was contrary to the philosophical foundations of Arts and Crafts values. Thus Mackintosh was exposed to a philosophical culture that, however refracted through other writings and through the commerce of daily life, was no longer unproblematical; a gulf had appeared between the 'common sense' of everyday criticism and the popular reception of art and the dialectical understanding that underpinned all new endeavours. In my final chapter I argue that Mackintosh's adherence to Associationist ideas may have formed an obstacle to the development of his work.

The tendency toward dialectical and synthetic thinking that had entered Scottish intellectual life was also reinforced at a more immediate and accessible level by the numerous activities and writings of Patrick Geddes, who shares several points of contact, both personal and intellectual, with Mackintosh. From a home ground in biology, this unresting and polymathic man made original contributions to education, town-planning and social geography.

I have delayed dealing with Mackintosh's immediate architectural experiences in order to stress the non-architectural aspects of his complete working environment. If I now turn to Glasgow's architects it is not to attempt an overview, but to pick out certain careers and buildings that relate to features of his life and work.

All writers are agreed that Mackintosh was closer to the English Arts and Crafts tradition and to post-Puginian concepts of craftsmanship and ornament than he was to the long-established classicizing traditions to be found in Glasgow. But the obvious difference can mask a more subtle similarity, for Glaswegian classicism grew from the Greek Revival of the early nineteenth century into an extravagant display of eclecticism and, in some cases, into a highly evolved originality. The work of Alexander 'Greek' Thomson, who was active from 1849 until his death in 1875, is important because it set the highest standards of composition, detail, learning and synthetic power. Thomson's churches, tenements and office buildings were among the largest structures in Glasgow, and

4 St Vincent Street Church, Glasgow (1859), by Alexander Thomson.

The mountain of masonry of St Vincent Street Church contains a hall beneath a hall; its cubic massing and spacing is developed continuously both within and without.

by some distance the most imposing in design. The villas he built in the countryside around the city surpassed any by his contemporaries. One of the finest of all his works, the St Vincent Street United Presbyterian Church (1859), stands on the hill opposite the School of Art; Mackintosh would have seen it every working day for many years (illus. 4). It has been described as 'a brilliantly original building which does not appear laboured or forced in any way . . . one of the truly great churches of the nineteenth century'.[25] It consists of a mountain of masonry that holds up a temple to the northern

5 Deeply incised decoration on the west porch of Thomson's St Vincent Street Church, Glasgow (1859).

The rigid power and emphatic modelling of the masonry of St Vincent Street Church is about as far from Mackintosh's treatment of similar features as it is possible to get; yet the thoroughness of these two architects is similar – everything is given the same degree of attention.

6 An exotic polychrome capital in the main hall of Thomson's St Vincent Street Church.

7 The end of a pew in the balcony of Thomson's St Vincent Street Church.

It would be difficult to find an architect other than Mackintosh whose attention to detail was as acute as that of Thomson. There are no stock mouldings or contractors' resolutions at St Vincent Street Church: everything is 'durchkomponiert'.

8 A cast-iron pillar penetrates the seating in the balcony of Thomson's St Vincent Street Church.

sky and, beside it, an extraordinary tower 'reminiscent of Indian architecture . . . a strange but brilliant ensemble of many diverse units wrought together into one magnificent climax'.[26] The mountain contains a hall for worship whose

> decoration throughout is exotic, owing much to classical Greece but also something to the barbaric splendour of Assyria or to the exotic sculptural forms of India. A new element is also present, in the form of decorative features which are derived from plants, and perhaps even shellfish, all of which are expressed in an original manner.[27]

Thomson can be described only loosely as 'Greek'; for although his starting-point was always scholarly, his work, especially in the immensely productive middle years, shows the intense interest he had in Egyptian, Hindu and other 'exotic' sources. Much of Thomson's interior work was carried out by Daniel Cottier, with whom he had a long-standing association.

As and when the need arose, Thomson also designed furniture. There is, for example, an immense cupboard by him, now in the Glasgow Art Gallery, in the form of a pylon such as appears on the side of the St Vincent Street Church; this cupboard is decorated in a mixture of classical and 'conventional' ornament. But what impresses one most in a Thomson building is the consistency that runs through all its parts, and which Cottier was able to draw down to the smallest details of the interior.

Thomson's ability to unify very diverse material was achieved throughout both structure and decoration. Structurally speaking, he employed a similar trabeated method of building in all his mature works, subjecting everything to this discipline and thereby achieving an idiom that was both individual and yet objectively determined. In detail, unity was achieved through a high degree of interchangeability, whereby features and motifs could work both as door and window elements, as courses or as pelmets, as porches or as bays. And this is true of all his buildings, large and small. This is an artistic strategy employed equally by Mackintosh; indeed, broadly considered, there are similarities between Thomson and Mackintosh that have nothing to do with style but have much to do with the methods employed by a synthesizing imagination. A number of writers have seen Thomson, like Mackintosh himself, as a proto-Modernist: 'It is clear that Thomson's creative development had reached a point where he was poised on the brink of a "modern" architecture . . . but he recoiled from the vision and left the development of a true modern architecture to a later generation'.[28] He has been linked in one direction with Karl Friedrich von Schinkel (1781–1841) and in the other with Frank Lloyd Wright (1869–1959). Today, however, when it is not quite so clear just what a 'true modern architecture' might be, we may want to see the problem with which Thomson wrestled – that of obtaining unity from diversity – as being much closer to Mackintosh's own concerns than might appear likely on stylistic grounds. Moreover, the balance that Thomson achieved between forceful individuality and objectivity was a balance that our architect also sought. Appropriately, one of the many prizes won by the young Mackintosh was the prestigious Alexander Thomson Travelling Scholarship, and the competition entries through which he gained further notice show the general influence of Glasgow's classicism.

Another architect of interest is William Leiper, who was active between 1845 and 1903; he represented the neo-Gothic tendency in Glasgow more completely than anyone else, and he was, as we have seen, involved in shipfitting. In addition to a number of churches he also built several grand houses and villas, on which he employed Glasgow's glass-artists and cabinet-makers. With Daniel Cottier as his collaborator, Leiper employed numerous Aesthetic Movement designers on such baronial prodigies as Colearn House (1870) and Cairndhu House (1872). However, his most remarkable structure in Glasgow is an exotic neo-Islamic-Byzantine-Venetian palazzo (completed 1889) built on Glasgow Green to house J. S. Templeton's carpet factory (illus. 9). This building was under construction when Mackintosh was serving his apprenticeship, and the contractors that Honeyman & Keppie were employing on the interior designs that Mackintosh made for them, and the firms for whom he was producing furniture designs, all had professional links with Leiper. Leiper also designed some furniture, among which is an astonishing painted and carved throne, exhibited today in The People's Palace, Glasgow. In 1891, along with several other of Glasgow's leading architects, he was appointed a Visitor at the School of Art. Though Leiper cannot be said to have had a

9 J. S. Templeton's carpet factory, Glasgow (1889), by William Leiper.

10 Part of the main façade of 'The Hat-rack' in St Vincent Street, Glasgow (1899), by James Salmon jnr.

The glass in the lantern of the Hat-rack was designed by Oscar Patterson, one of the finest Glasgow glass-artists of the time. Note how the window glazing comes right up to the stonework – a feature of Glasgow building that had been pioneered by Alexander Thomson.

stylistic influence on Mackintosh, like the much greater Thomson he existed as a local model for those who aspired to achieve an intense integration of ornament within the overall concept of a building.

Other individual architects and joint practices ranged over as wide a diversity of sources as Thomson and Leiper, but they did so in the course of designing successive buildings rather than simultaneously in one. The Salmons (grandfather, father and son) were a professional dynasty that, with various partners, made its mark on Glasgow over a period of fifty years. James Salmon the elder (1805–88) built churches, warehouses and the suburb of Dennistoun, as well as organizing the civic parks and gardens. The second Salmon was primarily a businessman but his son, the younger James (1874–1924), was apprenticed to William Leiper and went on to become an architect and decorative designer of great inven-

11 From Art Nouveau to proto-Modernism: Lion Chambers, Hope Street, Glasgow (1906), by James Salmon jnr.

Salmon's Lion Chambers is an early essay in reinforced concrete, with walls only a few inches thick.

tion. Gomme and Walker describe him as 'one of the few really original architects of his time in this country, a genuinely creative mind'.[29] Salmon was a fellow student and friend of Mackintosh and, like him, deeply concerned to integrate decoration and structure; the overall effect of a building like 'The Hat-rack' (142 St Vincent Street) of 1899 (illus. 10) is far closer to Parisian Art Nouveau than to the Glasgow Style. It contains stained glass by Oscar Patterson and many fine touches of detail. Salmon's Lion Chambers, Hope Street (1906), is a stark, geometric piece of work in reinforced concrete, with an eight-storey glass wall. This move from the ornate to the austere is similar to the evolution of Mackintosh's designs at the same time, and repeats the general tendency of the Arts Nouveaux to pass from the organic to the rectilinear (illus. 11).

Mackintosh's apprenticeship was with another such firm

of long-standing, that of John Honeyman (active 1862–83). In addition to being the master of a considerable practice, Honeyman was an expert on medieval building, with great experience of restoration and careful repair (notably, he restored the ancient abbey church on the island of Iona). He was also responsible for an unusual commercial building on Gordon Street, a sort of Venetian fantasia in iron and glass known as the Ca' d'Oro (1872; illus. 12). The combination of advanced technology and a detailed knowledge of old building types and methods that Mackintosh encountered as an apprentice should be reckoned a significant part of his professional education.

There is no architecture without clients. Who were the individuals, the chairmen of boards, the parish elders, the directors of companies, the magnates that were prepared to expend such very large sums of money on building? Something of their character can be seen in the diverse activities of J. S. Templeton, for whom William Leiper built the palatial factory. Templeton was a major manufacturer of carpets, whose firm had branches in Manchester, London, Melbourne and Montreal. He collected paintings and oriental *objets d'art*; furthermore, he was a member of the Board of the School of Art, to whose building fund he gave generously. He was thus one of those who commissioned Mackintosh's masterwork, and forms a personal link between one generation and the

12 The Ca' d'Oro, Gordon Street, Glasgow (1872), by James Honeyman, recently restored to its original simplicity.

next.[30] Such clients were members of a north-west British high bourgeoisie that was prepared to expend its considerable wealth on architecture and the visual arts, and which – all importantly – was willing to promote the newest talents. Though it is a matter that requires further research, in all likelihood the capital that was invested in these buildings was generated locally and locally controlled. The character of Glasgow's architecture in the late nineteenth century was bound to this financial autonomy through personal and institutional links: the decay of the Glasgow Style appears to have coincided with the growing control of the City of London's financial institutions over Scottish capitalism.

Glasgow's architectural world was indeed tight and little, in that its personnel was small and full of private and professional connections; but it was as wide-ranging in style as any to be found, and its technological support was broadly based and very advanced. It contained some very concentrated experience, and to search through the plan-chests of these offices would be to learn about nineteenth-century civic architecture at its best. It is important to stress that Mackintosh worked as much for institutional clients as for private patrons: his building in Renfield Lane, Glasgow, originally the offices of *The Daily Record* newspaper, is a typical piece of Glaswegian commercial building (illus. 13).

Even quite modest buildings of the period display an attention to detail and thoroughness of design that delights the visitor. But although the architectural culture in which Mackintosh was educated was among the best available, it lacked the passion for, and detailed knowledge of, the vernacular; that Mackintosh had to gain largely for himself through his encounters with the values of the Arts and Crafts Movement. He achieved it through reading, travel and incessant drawing.

From the standpoint of local and traditional culture, modernization is always experienced as loss, sometimes as a terrible wound. This is no less true of those centres of modernity in which the process is initiated, as it is of those margins where innovation is enforced. The forward drive is always accompanied by a retrospective longing for an earlier time. The culture of modernity is Janus-faced, and experienced as a tension:

13 Mackintosh's *The Daily Record* Offices, Renfield Lane, Glasgow (1897): glazed brick, masonry and iron.

Glasgow's narrow lanes created problems of lighting, hence the white glazing that throws light into what is a very constricted space. The green decorative accents on The Daily Record Offices prefigure Mackintosh's Northampton Style of 1916-7.

But in order to take part in modern civilization, it is necessary at the same time to take part in scientific, technical and political rationality, something which very often requires the pure and simple abandon of a whole cultural past . . . . There is the paradox: how to become modern and to return to sources.[31]

The artistic problems that this tension created were recognized as early as 1851. Ralph Wornum, writing in the *Illustrated Catalogue of the Great Exhibition*, argued:

The time has now gone by, at least in Europe, for the development of any particular or national style, and for this reason it is necessary to distinguish the various tastes that have prevailed through past ages, and preserve them as distinct expressions, or otherwise by using indiscriminately all materials, we should lose all expression . . . if all . . . is to degenerate into a uniform mixture of elements, nothing will be beautiful.[32]

The question of a distinct Scottish expression in architecture was under constant review in the latter part of the century; it not only influenced buildings, it gave rise to books. Studies of vernacular architecture appeared in parallel with buildings that attempted a modernized vernacular style: while David McGibbon and Thomas Ross were publishing their *Castellated and Domestic Architecture of Scotland* in five volumes between 1887 and 1892, architects such as James MacLaren and William Dunn were designing estate cottages and hotels in the Highlands that were based on careful study of local types. Robert Lorimer and other younger architects were learning from them and from English exemplars.[33]

Mackintosh was very much concerned with this question of 'distinct expression', and all his buildings speak of the vernacular even when departing from it. He described earlier Scottish architecture as the product of those who 'spoke in its pristine form our own language' and 'as indigenous to our country as our wild flowers', and a product of the modern rather than the Classical world.[34] It is quite clear that he regarded vernacular architecture as 'natural', and therefore (in Rousseau's and Ruskin's terms) as rational and good.

This concern was, and indeed still is, a cultural phenomenon that is typical of a society in the process of modernization. And since modernization is a continuous process, the search for 'vernacular' and 'traditional' validations of current practice is constantly with us. It is the root of those Arts and Crafts movements that came into being throughout Europe in the second half of the nineteenth century, and whose influence continues down to the present day. What makes Mackintosh's work so remarkable is that the balance between the neo-vernacular and the modern is so acutely struck. Indeed, if this is not seeming to be wise after the event, one can happily describe the local characteristics of Mackintosh's style as an early instance of what Kenneth Frampton has called a 'critical regionalism', that is to say, the search to comprehend the process of modernization within the terms of a specific locality and its architectural traditions.[35]

For an architect equally concerned with modernity, the use of vernacular models was appropriate because the vernacular is not a concept bound to any clear sense of history: it appears in architectural and poetic theory as a natural category, belonging to a 'timeless' folk. The adoption of vernacular models was, accordingly, a stage on the road to the abandonment of academic precedents. One got to the future by way of a deeper plunge into the past, where a 'rational', 'styleless' and 'natural' mirror was waiting to show the way to go. But the 'content' of Mackintosh's architecture, both literally and figuratively, can in no sense be described as traditional. The interiors, with their Symbolist imagery and atmosphere of nervous excitement, speak of an unbridled subjectivity that has nothing to do with vernacular values whatsoever.

Mackintosh's practical and intellectual environment may now be summarized in terms of binary oppositions, which include those between craft production and semi-industrial design, commercial and artistic education, and empirical and idealist aesthetics. Transposed into architectural terms, these were represented by such antinomies as the relation between structure and decoration, between the vernacular and the eclectic, and between local methods and modern technology. These oppositions were inscribed in the circumstances of a working life whose parameters were wider than architecture, though it was through architecture that Mackintosh sought to turn oppositions into a creative dialectic.

In the following chapters I attempt to follow the workings of this struggle toward a synthesis, through a reflection upon details of his practice.

2 Decoration into Structure: The Role of Drawing

Owen Jones's great volume, *The Grammar of Ornament* (1856), set out for the architects of the later nineteenth century the riches of the world's decoration. Jones's position in the Department of Science and Art (the institution that guided art education in Britain from its base in South Kensington, London) ensured that his book was very widely distributed; a copy was in the possession of every School of Art and major architectural practice in the country, and it was also extensively used elsewhere in Europe and America. It features in the intellectual biography of each significant designer of the period; there is every reason to assume that the young Mackintosh, like the young Le Corbusier, was well acquainted with its premises. In describing the nature of each recognized historical style and the decorative achievements of every known culture, it also threw down the challenge to create a new style for the new epoch; but it did so in terms that left the relation of decoration to structure ambiguous:

> Although ornament is most properly only an accessory to architecture, and should never be allowed to usurp the place of structural features, or to overload or to disguise them, it is in all cases the very soul of an architectural monument.[36]

Such statements epitomize the mid-nineteenth-century difficulty: ornament was held to be essential, even 'the very soul' of architecture; yet, at the same time, it was 'only an accessory'. Architectural decoration was that which through its associations and vivid sensual characteristics was seen to bear the meaning of a building – yet it had, in nearly every case, an arbitrary relation to the building's plan and structure. This was particularly the case in commercial building and housing. J. C. Loudon's *Encyclopaedia of Cottage, Farm and Village Architecture* (1833) illustrates a concept of ornament that a stylist in today's automotive industry will immediately recognize: in its illustrations a basic cottage (the engine, wheels and sub-frame assembly!) is transformed with different claddings into a miniature castle, an Elizabethan palace, a Chinese resthouse and a Buddhist *stupa*. In a similar manner, the young John Ruskin could restyle the same window opening for 'a man of feeling', a 'man of imagination' and 'a man of intellect'. Ornamental detail, because it struck the eye first and with vivid associations, was the primary signifier.[37] Davidoff and Hall (1987) credit Loudon's books and magazines with materializing the concept of individuality for the Victorian middle classes. His transformed cottages are the best early expression of the speculative builder's notions of Tudor, Georgian and 'traditional values'.

The only objection to these assumptions was voiced by architects who, on whatever grounds, demanded a congruence between all the parts of a building. Articulating that demand became the main business of architectural theory; and by the time of Mackintosh's youth a consensus had been achieved that broadly followed Pugin's dictum; this was that whatever 'style' was in question, 'all ornament should consist of enrichment of the essential structure of the building' (the important word here was 'essential'); this was epigrammatized into the saying (which Mackintosh himself is recorded as using) that 'construction should be decorated, and not decoration constructed'. And, at the same time, decoration was to be both 'appropriate and significant'.

The architects influenced by the Arts and Crafts movements opposed the notion of 'style' with that of 'character', and in this constellation of ideas 'style' meant 'copyism' and artifice, while 'character' was seen as natural and authentic. Indeed, character could be said to be without style, and the idea that the best – i.e. the natural, true vernacular – architecture was 'styleless' was current from the 1870s onward.[38] The touchstone of the building art became the vernacular cottage or barn, adorned only with the simplest craft and in a 'natural' relation to its surroundings.

Such a concept of quality could not directly give rise to innovative architecture, nor was that the intention, which was, in Ralph Wornum's words, to assert the 'distinct expression' of a nation or region, and to do so in a manner that was both rational and natural. Since these concepts are derived from the eighteenth-century philosopher Jean-Jacques Rousseau, such an architecture, being natural, would be morally sound, and the only valid expression of a 'natural' community. What this concept could do was purge the professional consciousness and public taste of the extremes of eclecticism, and introduce into design discourse the moralistic notions of 'honesty', 'truthfulness' and 'integrity'.[39]

Nevertheless, these doctrines remained in the province of 'art architecture'; they had little currency in the normal commercial practices and in the ramshackle apprenticeships that passed for architectural education. There, construction continued to be treated separately from decoration and, in so far as either was taught systematically, construction was learnt on the job and decoration in the Schools of Design. Mackintosh's apprenticeship was of this kind: by day he worked for the Honeyman practice and in the evenings at the Glasgow School of Art.

In normal commercial practice it was taken for granted that the major statement that a building could make was through its adornment. Thus decoration in general and architectural ornament in particular came to be seen as an important topic in its own right, and it developed an extensive and intensive discourse quite separate from building. What followed from this was a very large number of books and journals wholly or partly devoted to the arts of decoration, which were written with a seriousness that is unusual for the topic. Of these, the *Grammar* was pre-eminent.

Jones and his contemporaries expected a great deal from ornament, since by it 'we can judge more truly of the creative power which the artist has brought to bear on the work'; good ornament was not only 'a super-added beauty' but also 'an expression of the intention of the whole work'. Moreover, since decoration could be considered separately from structure, and could be shown to have developed autonomously, there was no reason why a new style of architecture should not arise led by decorative rather than structural designers:

> We therefore think we are justified in the belief that a new style of ornament may be produced independently of a new style of architecture; and moreover, that it would be one of the readiest means of arriving at a new style: for instance, if we could only arrive at the invention of a new termination to a means of support, one of the most difficult points would be accomplished.[40]

Seen from the standpoint of Jones and the theoreticians of decoration, Mackintosh's work looks like the culmination of *The Grammar of Ornament*'s project, which placed the renewal of architecture in the hands of the ornamentalist.

The *Grammar* was not, however, a simple compendium of styles; its overall intention was polemic:

> From the present chaos there will arise, undoubtedly (it may not be in our time), an architecture which shall be worthy of the high advance which man has made in every direction towards the possession of the tree of knowledge.

But how was this new style to be created?

> We think it impossible that a student fully impressed with the law of the universal fitness of things in nature, with the wonderful variety of form, yet all arranged around some few fixed laws . . . whatever type he may borrow from Nature, if he will dismiss from his mind the desire to imitate it, but will only seek to follow still the path which it so plainly shows him, we doubt not that new forms of beauty will more readily arise under his hand, than can ever follow from a continuation in the prevailing fashion of resting only on the works of the past for present inspiration.[41]

The 'path' was already indicated on page two of the great volume:

> That whenever any style of ornament commands universal admiration, it will always be found to be in accordance with laws that regulate the distribution of form in nature.

These laws were the findings of the life sciences. *The Grammar of Ornament* was, in fact, modelled upon the methods of comparative biology; thus the 'laws' of decoration have the implied status of the laws of life. The *Grammar* represented the extension of the cognitive monopoly of Positivism from science into the arts; and, ideologically, it asserted the necessity and 'natural' character of the complex of interests and ideas in which it was embedded. Thus Jones's new architecture that was to be developed out of a new decoration would be the style of a new epoch of victorious science and industry. Decoration was given a considerable task: to bring the built form of that epoch into being. The ideology of 'distinct expression' based upon national or regional styles and traditions was clearly at odds with Jones's modernism.

I have elsewhere described the nineteenth-century discourse of decoration as a struggle between this normative, scientistic concept of design (which, in time, was to lead to abstraction and the rejection of ornament), and a naturalistic and pictorial approach that derived its meanings not from 'laws' and the 'tree of knowledge', but from what Ruskin called 'local association and historical memory'.[42] We need to establish where Mackintosh stood in this evolving debate because of its architectural consequences, and to identify the medium through which an effective integration of decoration and structure could be brought about.

The most useful way into this maze is through an examination of Mackintosh's way of drawing, since that is the activity that was common to his building, his decoration and his painting; and it is clear from Francis Newbery's 1885 address that the Glasgow School of Art stressed its drawing curriculum:

All our great industries – whether of shipbuilding or house building, whether of engineering or machine making, whether of pattern-making or the higher art of painting – must first have their origin in drawing, and without this basis none of them can be established. The shipbuilder must first design his model; the architect his structure, the engineer his railway, his docks, or his bridges; the painter his sketch; and the designer his ideal, before he can begin his operations.[43]

Where design and decoration were concerned, drawing, and the teaching of drawing, had been the locus of a prolonged and fierce exchange of ideas conducted between two irreconcilable positions. On the one hand there was the drawing based upon the observation of 'natural facts', as put forward by Ruskin, and on the other the 'conventional' drawing proposed by the Department of Science and Art, whose principal theoretician was Christopher Dresser (1834–1904).

Dresser may be taken as the typical figure of the scientistic approach to design: a leading botanist and busy practising designer of great originality, he was also a pioneer enthusiast of the arts of Japan and of Art Nouveau. His opponent in these matters – Ruskin – is well recognized as the fountain-head of articulate and deeply considered anti-industrial theory. The positions taken by Dresser and Ruskin can be seen to align with the polar opposites, normative and critical, suggested above.

In describing the topic in this way, I am of course making a point of argument that can never fit exactly with any real example of practice. In a greater or lesser degree, the tendency to naturalism and abstraction was present in every nineteenth-century practitioner; the greatest pattern-designer of the period, William Morris, for example, while using botanically recognizable flower motifs based upon naturalistic drawing was also disposing these motifs according to 'conventional' order and in the required 'shallow' space. Ruskin wrote frequently, and eloquently, of the necessity of 'conventionalizing' forms for the purposes of manufacture; and Dresser (at least in his early wallpaper designs) employed naturalistic motifs in a very direct, even grotesque, manner. But the question at issue was this: From what source did a drawing for design spring? From Nature as perceived by the eye, or as known by science? The issue turned especially on the drawing of vegetation and flower-forms. Contrasting

14,15,16 Diagrams illustrating plant symmetries and sections from Christopher Dresser's *The Art of Decorative Design* (1862).

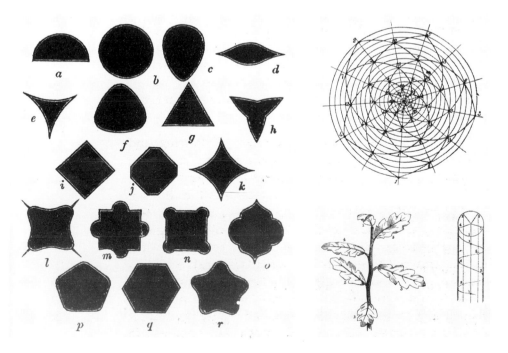

17 John Ruskin, *A Spray of Olive*, pencil and bodycolour, 1870. Ashmolean Museum, Oxford.

quotations and illustrations may suffice here. In an article of 1851 Edward Forbes noted that:

> The value to a designer of a scientific comprehension of the world is the insight it gives him into the possible variations of the original, and the inexhaustible sources of grace and beauty; whence so much that is new, and yet consistent, may be derived, toward the following out of nature's plan.[44]

This can be compared with Ruskin's comments in *The Eagle's Nest* (1872):

> In representing this organic Nature, Art has nothing to do with structures, causes or absolute facts, but only with appearances . . . in representing these appearances, she is more hindered than helped by the knowledge of things that do not externally appear. . . . You are, in drawing, to try only to represent the appearance of things, never what you know the thing to be. . . . My friends, let me very strongly recommend you to give up that hope of finding the principle of life in dead bodies . . . the artists has no concern with invisible structure, organic or inorganic.[45]

Forbes was one of the several leading life-scientists of the 1850s that were brought in to advise the Department of Science and Art. The scientific comprehension that he recommended required a manner of drawing that Dresser described as architectural, a 'representation of a more rigid character and analytic nature being necessary'; it involved 'at least an elementary knowledge of botany'. Richard Redgrave, another leading figure in the South Kensington Schools required that drawings be based on an 'ornamental analysis . . . diagrammatically flat to the eye'.[46] Nothing could be further from the delicacy of observation and rendering Ruskin demanded, based always upon respect for the 'natural facts' of vision.

The standard curriculum of the Department of Science and Art, known as the 'National Course of Instruction', worked all the way upward from simple outline drawing to shading, to copying from casts and, finally, to the life model. At all stages, a clear and 'determinate' line was expected from the student, and when shading was permitted it was to be done in an appropriately dry manner. Architectural students spent much of their time drawing classical ornament and learning a precise taxonomy of styles. Perspective and technical drawing was also required, to an exacting standard. This curriculum was deemed compulsory, but by the 1880s a good deal of local licence was allowed; government inspectors were themselves under the influence of other notions. The National Course provided the skeleton of the curriculum at the Glasgow School of Art, but under the direction of Francis Newbery it was followed without excessive dogma. In 1889, when Mackintosh had been five years at the School, the National Course ceased to be compulsory, and this change in the regulations led to the open introduction of a more Ruskinian approach to drawing and to the development of craft teaching along the lines of Arts and Crafts philosophy. Where the drawing of an apprentice architect was concerned, this meant the encouragement of a picturesque treatment of architectural subjects, an emphasis on old or vernacular structures, and the use of the notebook and sketch-pad as an aid to practical research.

The first courses on which Mackintosh enrolled (in 1884) were 'Painting ornament from the flat', and 'Painting ornament from the cast'; and his drawing courses progressed from

'Linear drawing with instruments' to 'Shading from the round'. He then studied architectural rendering and sketching with Thomas Smith and Alexander McGibbon, from whom he probably gained the very delicate handling that is such a feature of his early notebooks. What is missing in his drawing is any evidence of sustained practice in the life-class; but this was normal for design students.

The results of this mixed curriculum can clearly be seen in the drawings Mackintosh made during his Italian journey in 1891, after winning the Alexander Thomson Travelling Scholarship. A Ruskinian attention to details of ornament, executed with a tender touch, is matched with geometrically drawn constructional details which are often found together on the same sheet; picturesque watercolours exist side by side with rapid technical notations. These habits were continued in his later notebooks, but these are noticeably more linear in their treatment and more informal in their subject-matter, since they were for private use only (illus. 18,19).

In addition to this, Mackintosh had clearly studied, or taught himself, enough botany to become eventually a botanical illustrator of high attainment, with a detailed knowledge of his subject. Working as if to Forbes's prescription, by 1894 he had also learnt to invent 'new, and yet consistent' vegetation. Mackintosh's flower drawing, which provided the principal source of his decorative motifs, was based upon the South Kensington model of scientific comprehension.

But to these educational influences a third may be added. By 1889, when the curriculum became more experimental in character, the original empirical impetus of Ruskinian drawing was becoming thoroughly permeated by Symbolist idealism stemming from painters such as Edward Burne-Jones, and a more general aestheticism that included the cult of Japanese art. These tendencies were both present in the School of Art and in Glasgow's studios, and both stressed the linear rather than tonal values of drawing. The practice of drawing was the point at which all these distinct systems of value came together, in conflict.[47]

Where decoration was concerned, the site of the conflict was botanical study. This was not fortuitous; botany and the observation of flowers had acquired an emblematic significance in Victorian Britain. It was an activity that reached into many areas of life, both as a pastime and as a cult whose

18,19 Pencil and wash drawings by Mackintosh of St Cuthbert's Church, Holy Island, made in June and July 1901. Hunterian Art Gallery, University of Glasgow, Mackintosh Collection.

Some of the notebook drawings Mackintosh made during his stay on Holy Island in 1901 very neatly combine three aspects of his work: the architectonic, the structural and the decorative. These drawings were made with a hard (H) pencil on smooth cartridge paper – a most unforgiving combination. Close inspection suggests that Mackintosh normally drew in the main outlines with a very light touch indeed, after which – and with no more than a couple of trial attempts – he produced the final version of his lines in a much firmer hand. Nowhere is there any sign of erasure. The touches of colour wash have their counterpart in the white interiors as patches of enamel or coloured glass, or as stencils made in much lighter tones.

ST. CUTHBERT'S CHURCH
HOLY ISLAND
M   JUNE   1901

S. CUTHBERT'S CHURCH
HOLY ISLAND
1901

symbolism fed the interlocking discourses of decoration and femininity. Even serious scientific authors, such as M. J. Schleiden, included chapters on 'the aesthetics of the vegetable world' in his popular writings, in which he justified the Positivism of modern botany on the grounds that only exact science could reveal the mystery and beauty of the natural world.[48] The common term for this blending of natural history with drawing for decoration, was 'art botany'.

There is no doubt that art botany and the cult of the flower, with its manifold symbolisms, were a major part of Mackintosh's mental formation during these early years. The flower came to represent for him the transcendent possibilities of architecture, a supra-mundane perfection, as his lecture notes on 'Seemliness' (1902) reveal:

> Art is the flower – Life is the green leaf. Let every artist strive to make his flower a beautiful living thing – something that will convince the world that there may be – there are – things more precious – more beautiful – more lasting than life . . . you must offer real, living – beautifully coloured flowers – flowers that grow from but above the green leaf – flowers that are not dead – are not dying – not artificial – real flowers – you must offer the flowers of the art that is in you – the symbols of all that is noble – and beautiful – and inspiring – flowers that will often change a colourless leaf – into an estimated and thoughtful thing.[49]

When Mackintosh left the School in 1892 he had spent eight years there in part-time study, most of them in drawing. The method of drawing that he was able to bring to architecture and its decoration had been summed up the previous year by C. F. A. Voysey in the very first issue (April 1893) of *The Studio*:

> To go to Nature is, of course, to approach the fountainhead, but a literal transcript will not result in good ornament; before a living plant a man must go through an elaborate process of selection and analysis . . . if he does this, although he has gone directly to Nature, his work will not resemble any of his predecessors; he has become an inventor . . . we are at once relieved from restrictions of style and period, and can live and work in the present with laws revealing always fresh possibilities.

20 Edward Hornel and George Henry, *The Druids Bringing Home the Mistletoe*, oil on canvas, 1890. Glasgow Museums and Art Galleries.

21 Mackintosh, *Sea Pinks*, pencil and watercolour, 1901. Hunterian Art
Gallery, University of Glasgow, Mackintosh Collection.

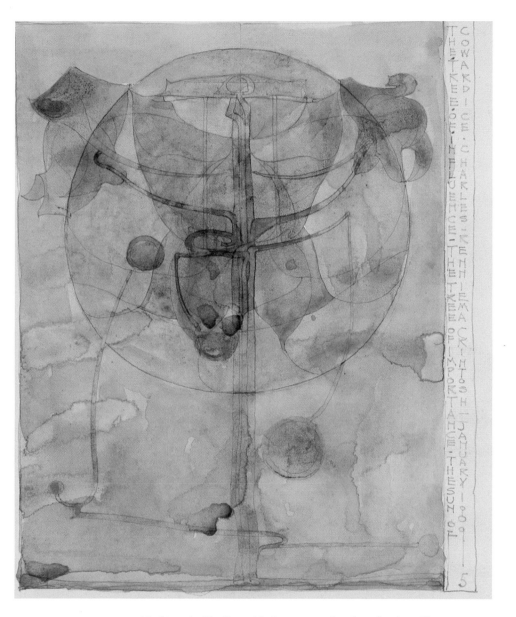

22 Mackintosh, *The Tree of Influence*, pencil and wash, 1895. Glasgow School of Art.

23 Mackintosh, *The Tree of Personal Effort. The Sun of Indifference*, pencil
and wash, 1895. Glasgow School of Art.

This process of selection and analysis leading to invention, whose combinatorial method is based, essentially, upon a 'scientific comprehension' of Nature, is the outcome of Owen Jones's 'laws of the distribution of form in nature', which all ornamental artists were to follow. That is to say, his drawing practice, other than technical, was based upon decorative, not architectural, premises. The importance of this cannot be over-stressed. Moreover, there was in his work from 1893 onward, a super-added quality, a power of imaginative metamorphosis.

The development of this power was intimately linked to Mackintosh's encounter with the Macdonald sisters and their friends in the coterie of 'The Roaring Camp'.[50] The fusion of numerous graphic influences effected in the work of Margaret and Frances Macdonald is both modish and creatively original. *The Yellow Book*, Continental Symbolism, Japanese and Celtic influences all came together in their work, but their original quality resided in the peculiar ability of the Mac-donalds to transform bodies into vegetation and vegetation into bodies; their drawings and paintings are full of inter-changeable forms and visual puns, frequently of a sexual character. Though this is a feature of much Art Nouveau, it is the main theme in their work. There is nothing as extreme as Frances Macdonald's little painting *The Pond* of November 1894 in all the available reproductions of French and Belgian Symbolism; nor is there anything in the work of the estab-lished Glasgow painters, such as Hornel and Henry, that licensed them to be so adventurous. What the Macdonalds and their friends effected, albeit on a small scale, was a large step away from both the Positivist foundation of 'conven-tional' drawing and from Ruskinian naturalism, toward a new world of subjective idealism and the neo-occult. This was a dialectical shift of some magnitude and consequence.

Of the exact stages by which Mackintosh entered and assimilated himself to this imaginative world, most are likely to remain hidden; but the results are plain enough when we investigate them. We are dealing with a rising spiral of mutual emulation and interaction, fuelled by sexual entanglements, Symbolist literature and an attempt (inspired by feminism) to redefine gender roles. This metamorphic and highly conven-tionalized style is the product of the School of Art curriculum with its three-way dialectic, infused by the intellectual and personal interests of the group.

I have described above the most important sources of Mackintosh's drawing; but to these is added a graphic transparency, whereby the profiles of forms are visible through those intervening; new forms are generated either by isolating the resultant shape, or by applying a wash that distinguishes one area from another. This practice connects to architectural drawing through the use of tracing paper. It is also a device in ship design, in which successive hull profiles are laid over one another. Both the formal drawings and the notebooks are full of examples of this transparency; it is perhaps most clearly seen in the flower paintings (illus. 21). It enables typical lines to be superimposed on one another to form new configurations. He – and, we must add, Margaret and Frances Macdonald – were able to transform one motif into another within the same mesh of lines and to develop both variety and consistency to an unusual degree. Graphic habits so richly developed enable the hand to work by itself, while freeing the mind for preconscious fantasy and pure play. This method and imagination leads to results that are both constructible and metaphorical. Indeed, one might say that the method was itself a metaphor, because the process of analysis, selection and transformation, and the combinatorial elaboration of the results, is a metaphor for the generative power of Nature as given us in a scientific comprehension.

The significance of this coming together is made clear when we analyse two small paintings of the period. From the care spent upon its lettering and the elaborate full title, the *Tree of Influence* (dated January 1895) appears to have been regarded by the artist as important. This, and the closely associated *Tree of Personal Effort*, have often been regarded as enigmatic. Neither, strictly speaking, were designs for decoration, but both are very closely associated with the decorative work of those years. Their format and character is also similar to *The Pond* and other works that appeared in *The Magazine* in 1894, and to a number of completed designs. If we analyse them with the foregoing in mind they seem less like locks and more like keys.

The Tree of Influence (illus. 22) consists of four main elements; a ground of dull purple wash (whose knowingly haphazard application is itself worth some study), a 'sun' laid over it in a watery red, a 'tree' in viridian green, and three connected billowing shapes of dull lilac. The tree and the

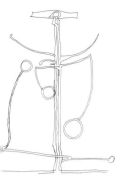

24 A tracing from
Mackintosh's *The
Tree of Influence*,
1895.

25 A tracing from
Mackintosh's *The
Tree of Influence*,
1895.

26 A tracing from
Mackintosh's *The
Tree of Personal
Effort*, 1895.

three shapes are related by rhyming, curving lines across the face of the sun; some of these curves mark the boundaries of the colours, others are left to provide rhythmical accompaniment. The full title (rarely given in books) is inscribed in a band down the right-hand side: 'The Tree of Influence – The Tree of Importance – The Sun of Cowardice – Charles – Rennie – Mackintosh – January 1895'. The tree and the two shapes, traced out (illus. 24–5), immediately set in train associations and connotations that are very hard to resist. The shapes become a cuirass, or the bodice of a dress with short bouffant sleeves; the tree stands before us as a hieroglyphic human figure (is it also a crucifix?), almost certainly male, an implement that is part hammer and part a pair of pincers, and an object in wrought-iron. The separation of the two structures by colour suggests that this reading is the one intended, though it may be that the lines were drawn with some measure of preconscious fantasy.

The companion piece, *The Tree of Personal Effort, The Sun of Indifference* (illus. 23), does not so easily divide into 'male' and 'female' elements, but it contains several graphic inventions of similar richness. The three trunks, or columns, are interwoven with a structure that bears a striking resemblance to a diagram of the female reproductive system; the volume created by the 'sun' in its interaction with the curves suggests a pregnancy (illus. 26). The upper area contains lip-like forms which themselves enclose a winged seed that is also a bird; the flowery shapes have further sexual associations. Both works contain what in architectural terms we would call 'immured figures'; and this half-concealed, half-opened imagery is to be found all through Mackintosh's decorative work and, to a less obvious degree, in his architecture and even furniture. It is a product both of Mackintosh's more (or less) conscious intentions, and of his drawing method.

Something must be said about the curious titles of these two little paintings. In the absence of any other evidence I assume them to be a coded self-revelation, half-serious and half-playful, in which 'effort' is set against 'indifference' and 'influence' against 'cowardice'; and that in each case the tension is expressed in an eroticized dualism of 'male-female', 'upright-curved', 'slack-taut', and so on. They belong to that world of the neo-occult, in which the soul is conceived as a tree growing out of the material world and into the realm of the spirit.

Graphic emblems of Trees of Knowledge – both Good and Evil – appear in eighteenth-century Rosicrucian literature; the works of Jacob Boehme contain a representation of the soul as a tree growing up into a circular 'sun' of Paradise and 'the light of majesty'.[51] There are reports of a Rosicrucian community in Glasgow at this time, though this may actually have been a Theosophical society. There was certainly a large Spiritualist Association (founded in 1867), and it is entirely possible that the Macdonald sisters had some involvement in one or more of these circles.[52] Another, and more immediate, connection may be with Patrick Geddes's Outlook Tower in Edinburgh. This building had been obtained by Geddes in 1892 and laid out as a sort of theatre of knowledge, through which disciplines and institutions could be given new relations. Among the charts and diagrams on its walls and windows was an *Arbor Saeculorum* – a Symbolist diagram of human development, complete with spirals, sphinxes and a phoenix. However, this remains conjectural, since we do not know of any direct link between Geddes and Mackintosh at this period.[53] At all events, we can assume that the titles of the two Mackintosh paintings make allusions to the private cults of the Glasgow Four.[54] Herbert MacNair affirmed in the context of his own related design, *The Tree of Knowledge*, 'that not a line was drawn without purpose, and rarely was a single motive employed that had not some allegorical meaning'.[55]

Mackintosh's decorative imagery, his treatment of materials and the manner in which the interiors of his buildings were made to relate to their exteriors was, indeed, allegorical. In 1894 the allegorical intention could only find expression in drawing and painting; but ten years later he had learnt to embody it in an entire building.

These drawings by Mackintosh and others of this period, and related drawings by the Macdonald sisters and Herbert MacNair, are a rich source of decorative imagery, and their forms recur throughout the next ten years in innumerable combinations and variations. All four borrowed and paraphrased one another, and these inventions were further paraphrased (or copied) by other contributors to the Glasgow Style. The 'tree' drawings impinge directly upon designs in such works as *Part Seen, Imagined Part* of 1896 in which the female figure emerges out of the stems of a 'plant' below it.

We note also the presence of a 'sun', a motif to be found in many of the Macdonald drawings. This in turn leads onto the various decorative designs for the tea-rooms, such as *The Wassail* (1900), which are related to numerous other designs in which curves originating in vegetation turn into motifs related to drapery and vice versa, and creating through their interweavings further images.[56] Metaphors and visual puns proliferate as if in a dream; did this drawing not exhibit remarkable linear control and conscious method we might call it a fantasia of the unconscious. One can identify and classify a range of motifs – birds, seeds, tulips, leaf-spears and so on; but these are not fixed elements, since all turn into one another and into something else (illus. 27, 28, 29).

The roses that appear all through the period of the Glasgow Style are likewise constructed from enmeshed curves that relate more to one another than to any real flower, and which provide an example of the method in miniature. We note that these roses seem to contain eyes, lips and other sensitive body parts. Those designed by Mackintosh and Margaret

27 Mackintosh, *A Hawk*, pencil drawing, October 1896. Hunterian Art Gallery, University of Glasgow, Mackintosh Collection.

28 Detail of a
bedroom
cupboard designed
by Mackintosh in
1901. Hunterian
Art Gallery,
University of
Glasgow,
Mackintosh
Collection.

29 Detail of a
living-room
cupboard designed
by Mackintosh in
1901. Hunterian
Art Gallery,
University of
Glasgow,
Mackintosh
Collection.

30,31,32
Comparative
tracings of roses by
Glasgow Style
artists.

Macdonald are clearly more elaborate and energetic than any to be found in the rest of the Glasgow designers, not excepting Frances Macdonald and Herbert MacNair. The single most elaborate rose-fantasy of them all is probably the pair of gesso panels by Margaret Macdonald made for the 'Rose Boudoir' at the Turin Exhibition (1902). In the first, *The White Rose and the Red Rose*, two cloaked female figures that lean towards one another create, or are created from, a rose-like configuration of lines; in the second, *The Heart of the Rose* (illus. 60), the swirl of lines produces a new rose within the first, which contains a child. Here the intensely female, even gynaecological, character of the motifs is openly stated and the design becomes both metaphor and sign. In the hands of lesser designers the excess became mawkish, or the rose is merely a symbol of an indefinite kind (illus. 30–2).[57]

This manner of drawing irrupts into the architectural work in such examples as the perspective study for Queen Margaret's Medical College of 1894. This building is set in a garden of unusually energetic and excited trees and shrubs; the two female figures transform the scene into a Pre-Raphaelite convent (that these are female medical students at that date is in itself interesting). By 1895 the fervour begins to be incorporated into the structure of the early buildings, as in the swelling posts of the roof-truss in the hall of the Martyr's Public School, and the ironwork of its banisters. At the same time, the metalwork and poster designs of the other three members of The Four begins to expand in scope and ambition, and to form a recognizable decorative style. By the end of 1899 and the opening of the first phase of the new School of Art building, what had begun in drawing had extended itself across every area of the decorative arts and into architectural composition to such a degree as to begin a resolution of the relation between structure and ornament that Owen Jones had outlined forty years before.

A brief comparison of roof timbers from the buildings of these five years helps to show the growing unity between structure and decoration that Mackintosh's method of drawing fostered: we pass from the decorated king- and queen-post trusses of 233 St Vincent Street to the composite truss of Queen's Cross Church with its 'tree of life' emblem (an emblem upon an emblem), to the extravaganza of the School of Art Museum with its 'crossbow' timbers, to the highly eccentric roof of the Life Studio (illus. 33). In the final example, the drawing of decorative motifs has been superseded by their construction.

Another very clear example of this unity is the design for a domino table, possibly intended for the Argyle Street Tea Rooms (1897). Here the supports of the table form a void in the familiar 'tulip' shape, and the plan of the table bears a marked resemblance to the flower-symmetry plans recommended as models by Dresser and the other art-botanists (illus. 34). The spread of graphic ideas into construction is well illustrated by the metamorphosis of the grids of coloured tiles that are a feature of the School of Art, but which pass over into three dimensions five years later for the furniture of Hill House (having also appeared in a stand for the 1901 Glasgow Exhibition and in a display cabinet for the 1902 Turin Exhibition); from 1906 onward, this grid becomes the primary organizing element. In other cases, constructional motifs carry over from furniture into architectural timberwork and vice versa. This is particularly the case in certain tables, which, as Roger Billcliffe has observed, 'miniaturise' the forms of the Library of the School of Art.

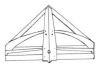

Some of these graphic/architectonic themes can be identified easily, but others are more deeply buried in the overall composition. The balanced asymmetry of the façades of the School of Art have usually been seen as a meeting-point between the neo-vernacular and modernism; but seen from the perspective of decoration they embody the principles of Mackintosh's approach to drawing. The metaphorical element is not confined to decorative detail – such as the crease in the keystone of the east entrance – but expands into the *contrapposto* stance of each façade. Consider, for example, the relation between the projecting windows of the Library on the west façade with similar windows to the rear of the building, which are recessed. Consider also the wide-radius curves in the vertical stonework that appear beside the Library windows and elsewhere on the west façade, which then come round to the front of the building to soften the edges of the great Studio windows (illus. 35, 36, 37).

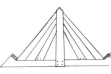

In still more general terms we can identify typical curves and characteristic proportions that pass easily, though with appropriate modifications, from small scale to large and back again. These all have a graphic origin, and appear at first as

33 Sequence of comparative sketches by the author of roof trusses to be found in Mackintosh's buildings in Glasgow.

This sequence of roof trusses shows an ever greater divergence from standard designs. From top to bottom: king-post and queen-post trusses in 233 St Vincent Street (1894); a composite truss in Queen's Cross Church (1897); the 'crossbow' timbers of the School of Art's Museum (1897-8); and the eccentric timbering of the School of Art's Life-class Studio (1897-8).

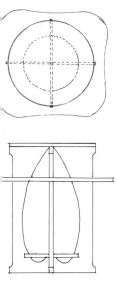

34 Plan and elevation of a domino table designed by Mackintosh, c. 1897.

The elevation of this domino table reveals how the inner curves of the supports were designed to form a 'tulip' motif.

motifs or as decorative typifications of natural form, but take on three dimensions to become central elements of a unified form-language. At this level of development, the idea of the motif is transformed from that of the stable pattern element into something far more akin to the motif in musical composition; that is to say, it becomes the essential material, one that is subject to variation and transformation, whose adventures are the content of the work. At the risk of pushing this analogy too far, I assert that Mackintosh's motifs are comparable to the *leitmotiven* of Richard Wagner, for they are conceived as metaphors from the beginning, and recur at strategically significant intervals, but transformed to give new meaning. This analogy is not arbitrary, since Wagner's compositional methods, tone colour and artistic character are among the foundations of Symbolism; and, as in music, the motif and its adventures cannot be separated from the architectonic organization of the whole work. Moreover, in 'Seemliness', Mackintosh himself was happy to use the analogy with musical composition when describing 'the deep vibration of some unifying undertone' that identifies true architecture.

Since drawing for decorative design was an activity loaded with ideological suggestions, what does the method and its imagery imply? In the first place, it constituted what is now called a 'shape-grammar', based on the scientific comprehension of Nature as developed by art botany and 'conventional' drawing. It consisted of a set of graphic elements from which motifs could be created, and also a set of combinatorial methods from which a virtually infinite series of ensembles could be constructed. By these means a designer could claim to be following what were understood to be the principles rather than the forms of Nature, and thus become free from History and 'copyism'. The grammar was an attempt to ensure a unity-from-diversity, by which one might 'live and work in the present with laws always revealing fresh possibilities'.

The analogy is biological, and the pattern of thinking derives from comparative anatomy as much as from botany. Cuvier's very widely published researches of the 1830s had established a principle of 'correlation of parts' among living organisms. As a long-dead creature can accurately be recon-

35 South (rear) façade of the Glasgow School of Art: Library extension (1907-9).

37 West façade of Mackintosh's Library (1907-9) at the School of Art.

36 Sketch-plan by the author of Mackintosh's School of Art.

What is negative on one side becomes positive on the other: this sketch-plan indicates the position of the cylindrical forms high on the west façade of the School of Art that are taken around the corner to the north façade (top), where they frame the Studio windows and the alternation of projecting and recessed windows on the west and south façades. In such cases it is hard to separate the architectonic from the decorative.

structed from a few fossil remains so, from the details of a balustrade, two joists and a window-frame, one might reasonably infer the entire building. Gottfried Semper had seen in this zoological model a lesson for architects, a solution of the problem of 'how to invent'; and it is this concept that reappears in Voysey's notion of 'laws' and 'possibilities'.[58] These are the origins of an 'organic' design theory; and though Mackintosh evinced no specific interest in the biological analogy, it is his design methods that provide the most convincing illustration of an idea that had become, by 1890, part of the professional assumptions of every advanced architect.[59] In this sense, the drawing may be said to be the foundation of a quasi-scientific method of invention.

But the drawing is not simply a shape-grammar; it is not only formal motifs that are invented, but an imagery of immured figures, a system of metaphors of the human body and vegetation so extensive as to constitute a developed iconography. This creates a fervour of metamorphosis that is akin to the dream-work of the unconscious. Thus the method leads directly into the significance, which was, in some general sense, a set of connected metaphors of subjectivity, sublimation and transcendence. This transcendentalism was not opposed to the Positivistic attitudes of the South Kensington School and its 'laws' and 'principles' modelled upon the natural sciences; it was its necessary counterpart and the resolution of its problem of meaning.

As I have already shown, art botany and the cult of the flower were topics heavy with implications; nor was this confined to the arts, since scientific botany itself was permeated with Symbolist ideas. This is not the historical Associationism of Ruskin's *Proserpina* (1879); it can be seen in scientific publications such as *The Journal of Botany*, which in 1863 published a translation of Goethe's *Metamorphosis of the Plants*, and later the anonymous fragment known as *Die Natur* (in 1869). This latter piece, which had emanated from Goethe's circle at Weimar many years before, speaks of Nature as 'sole artist; from the simplest material she passes to the extremest diversity'.[60] These ideas passed into art botany and the cult associations of rose and lily, sunflower and chrysanthemum that the Aesthetic Movement encouraged. This quasi-biological unity was developed in and through Mackintosh's method of drawing, while across the Atlantic it formed the root of Frank Lloyd Wright's 'organic' architectural theory; and it even appeared in a marked fashion in Louis Sullivan's *System of Architectural Ornament* (1924), with its 'parallelism . . . between man and nature, and between man and his works'.[61] What this transcendental idealism offered was a way out of the loss of meaning that Positivism threatened to inflict. Indeed, the inner meaning of art botany and the 'laws' and 'possibilities' was, that when the works of man have the infinite variety and unerring fitness of Nature, human perfection through progress will have been achieved. This is the mystical contraband in the Positivist's luggage.

> The knowledge that he invokes in order to interpret the meaning of positive knowledge does not itself meet the standards of the positive spirit . . . it is only through metaphysical concepts that positivism can render itself comprehensible.[62]

Nor is there any doubt that in the work of The Four, and most especially in the Mackintosh/Macdonald 'white interiors', this transcendental idealism was suffused with an erotic tension – a tension that was a common feature of the period, but which in Mackintosh was brought to the highest level in invention and integrated into the structure of buildings.

This idealism was in flat contradiction to the neo-vernacular doctrines of the Arts and Crafts Movement to which, in other respects, Mackintosh subscribed; and irreconcilable with the empiricism and 'common sense' philosophy that underpinned its Associationist aesthetics. His idealism is the mark of the Positivist and Utilitarian attitudes of the nineteenth century reversing into their dialectical opposite – transcendental fervour. This fervour was noted from the very first:

> Here we found the strangest mixture of puritanically severe functional forms and lyrical sublimation of the practical. . . . Here were mysticism and aestheticism, although far removed from the Christian sense of the former word, and with a strong sense of heliotrope, and a feel of well-cared-for hands, and of delicate sensuality.[63]

English contemporaries regarded this perceived quality as 'unhealthy', 'revolting' and 'diseased'. Pevsner, writing years later, responded in the same vein: 'Everything is extremely seductive, but far from pure'.[64] Coming again to the architectural decoration and the white interiors, with a sensibility that has been half-consciously formed by the very objects to which it now addresses itself, we find the eroticism less questionable and the emotional fervour closer to our taste. We may be more impressed (and not always favourably) with the logical consistency and the all-encompassing ambition of the style. This rigour and desire for totality, proper to the work of imagination and fantasy, appears to be escaping into real space and real life.

My intention here has been to stress the role of drawing in the creation of this style; to show that the drawing methods that Mackintosh developed derived from the discourse of decoration, rather than architecture, and that this had significant bearing on the innovative nature of his buildings, since it enabled him to resolve the nineteenth-century antimony of decoration and construction. Thus Mackintosh's drawing embodied that faculty of invention – the unity of reason with emotion and of science with imagination – that he demanded of architecture and to which the lecture on 'Seemliness' was addressed. In the 'Seemliness' notes we find that 'The architect . . . depends very greatly for his success upon a kind of instinct, a synthesis, or integration of myriads of details and circumstances of which he cannot be directly very conscious but the appreciation of which makes the master in every profession'.[65] His drawing was the vehicle of his integration.

38 Emblem on the title-page of Walter Crane's *The Basis of Design* (1898).

Crane's art and writings, like those of W. R. Lethaby, represent an attempt at English symbolist design theory that was never able to escape from its Arts and Crafts 'common-sense' origins. The angel bearing a torch is clearly a cousin of those painted by Edward Burne-Jones. The general form of this emblem is that of a Tree of Life or, perhaps, of a chalice. Whereas Crane illustrated his concept by drawing it as an emblem, Mackintosh arrived at his metaphors through drawing.

3 The Poetics of Workmanship

I have described Mackintosh's drawing as a medium of integration, the medium in which diverse, and even contradictory, aspects of his education could be synthesized, and the vehicle by which all elements of the building, from the smallest to the largest, could be unified. But drawing is merely a stage on the road to realization. In this chapter my concern is with the treatment of materials.

Our responses to materials, to our most favoured or most loathed surfaces, textures and grains, and the associations they arouse, are keys to the inner life. To use these keys fully and confidently would require a 'psychoanalysis of workmanship' not unlike that produced by Gaston Bachelard for the elements of earth, air, fire and water.[66] Our relationship to structures is infused with bodily expectations – of weight, tension, impetus and rest. The joined members of a frame, the posts of a truss, the joists, beams and purlins reproduce for us our skeletal imagining. There are secret satisfactions in good timberwork: it answers the desire for structural logic and empathetically reinforces the sense we have of ourselves as being coherent bodies. Thus the manner in which a building is put together, or an interior or piece of furniture constructed, and the many ways in which materials are made to show forth their natures, are potent elements in the meaning of the whole. For the same reason, the hiding of structure and the cloaking or disguising of materials can be full of significance. To these psychic considerations we must add the mass of assumptions and ideological rationales that had developed during the nineteenth century, and which were directly related to issues of workmanship, craft and methods of manufacture. What we observe in Mackintosh is a range of attitudes to materials and their joinings that follow a definite pattern.

Let me express this in simple terms: the more private the situation, the more likely a material is to be disguised; and the more public, the more likely it is to be displayed. This, as we shall see, broadly correlates with associations of gender, whereby a rough 'masculine' exterior with clearly displayed materials and an 'expressed' structure contains a smooth 'feminine' interior. Interior *public* spaces, such as halls, libraries and stairways, mediate between these two extremes. The interactions between different materials and their working, and their relation to the several kinds of spaces, can be shown to reveal patterns that I will call a 'poetics'. By this I mean a consistent and orderly set of associations deliberately evoked in order to body forth a coherent value system. The movement from the outside to the inside of a building, and the return to the outside, enacts this system in the form of an allegorical journey.

To use the terms 'masculine' and 'feminine' is tendentious. I hope it is understood that I am adopting the meanings these terms conveyed at the time in question. The association between femininity and the domestic interior (and, by extension, all the arts of decoration) remained constant in design in the nineteenth century; those interiors that were thought to be 'masculine' – studies, libraries, club rooms and so forth – were, with few exceptions, designed in an uncluttered style that was meant to signify masculinity. On the other hand, the more a space was intended for use by women, the more pretty and decorative it was. The poetics that I seek to trace through Mackintosh's use of materials was part of a wider and more general redefinition of public, domestic and intimate space. This redefinition was part of the project of the 'Arts Nouveaux', but in Mackintosh's work it received its most complete architectural realization. Any shift in the relations between public and private spaces entailed a redifferentiation of gender; in a Mackintosh building it asserted a version of the 'feminine' as the centre of spiritual innovation fired by an idealized erotic imagery. This femininity was not, by contemporary standards, fully emancipatory because it still equated woman with inferiority and eroticism; but it was a necessary first step away from identifying women with domesticity.

I propose to investigate this 'poetics' first from the outside inward, because that is how we encounter a building and make our journey from the public to the private. In the final chapter I will reverse this track and re-emerge into public space. Thus we make a beginning with walls and with stone, as it is formed around doors and windows.

Any study of Mackintosh's use of stone must be centred on the School of Art, a building that manages to be both powerful and tender; many of its details are simple, but they are very various and, in some cases, unexpected. I am not concerned here with the whole architectural composition as such, but only with the artistic effect of its stonework detailing. Walls are, of course, the elements of building least susceptible to innovation and fancy; for Mackintosh they were those parts of the design that most fully retained their links with vernacular tradition in terms of the methods used, the details and the overall balance of their appearance.

For the School of Art Mackintosh used a local stone known as Givnock. Givnock is a hard, fine-grained sandstone that resists weathering well and will take sensitive carving; in the Glasgow environment it soon becomes dark and in the winter it tends to attract a greenish algae, so that the north façade of the School, for example, can look unwashed. For his other stone buildings Mackintosh used a deep pink-orange sandstone that is common in Scotland. The body of the School's walls and piers is mostly composed of rough stone and brickwork and, following vernacular examples, the walls are usually thick. Finely dressed stone is reserved for special locations, such as the Library façade and the north front; massive masonry is kept for particular emphasis. But between them are semi-regular 'plain-work' areas that are more or less featureless. These are all conventions sanctioned by local custom, but Mackintosh took them to a new pitch of refinement or excess.

An example of excess is to be found on the east elevation, where an octagonal form – that appears to be, but is not, a stairwell – is slotted into the mass of the building above the entrance. This 'tower' rises from a projection modelled in smooth ashlar with curvilinear features and string-courses, while the projection – which is actually a bay window for a staff office – rests on an enormous cubic block, one of the largest pieces of stone to be found in the whole building (illus. 39). Projecting features of this general type are common in Scottish castles and tower houses, but these are normally supported with some attempt at tapered delicacy. We know from his sketch-books that Mackintosh had studied such

features in detail. Were this block not placed with a minute sense of visual balance, it would appear very crude. Its visual function is to reassure us that the 'tower' is adequately supported and to anchor the asymmetric balance of the whole façade. It is interesting to note that in a drawing made in 1897 (before construction began), this block does not appear; its place is taken by a small window.[67] The block appears to be one of those features that Mackintosh improvised in the course of building and which, all taken together, added significantly to the overall cost. It is essentially a device that is there to help create a good 'gestalt' by emphasizing both the cubic grid pattern of the whole building and the security of its fabric; it performs no serious mechanical function.

This kind of feature is to be met with all over Mackintosh's buildings. A similar example of 'crude' construction appears in the Martyr's Public School of 1895–6, where a small window high up in the stairwell is supported by a massive sill, which is itself supported on enormous brackets (illus. 48). This is a standard device of village architecture enlarged far beyond what one would normally expect to find. Likewise, the double beams in the Queen's Cross Church are supported on enormous blocks, reiterating the already over-emphatic rectangularity of the pillars on which they rest

40 Detail showing a capital supporting double beams in Mackintosh's Queen's Cross Church, Glasgow (1900).

(illus. 40). In all these cases, stone is being used to exaggerate the mass and weight well beyond what it actually has to bear.

Something like the opposite effect is to be found on the west façade of the School of Art, designed and built eight years later, where the treatment of the entrance suggests apparent movement (illus. 41). The two courses above the keystone are carved and dressed into a band that takes up the wide curves seen on the façade and the entrance, but reverses them. The interplay of shadow gives a sense of a horizontal rotary movement that is at variance with the vertical tension of the main masses. This is picked up by the forms either side of the door that look like revolving cylinders. The keystone of the entrance is no more than a rectangular recess that in certain conditions of light appears to contain a further 'roller'. The result is to induce unease in the onlooker. The whole entrance protrudes rather than recedes, and it is framed by a set of stepped mouldings that have no clear precedent known to me (illus. 42). There is a mannerist element in this, which thwarts the expectations of the eye and the interior sense of static mass; it looks backward to Mannerism and forward to Art Deco, and is even, in a sense, post-modern before it is modern.

A similar, but less extreme, example can be found in one

41 Main entrance on the west front of the School of Art (1907-9).

42 Stepped mouldings above the main entrance to Mackintosh's School of Art.

43 Entrance to Mackintosh's office building in Renfield Lane, Glasgow, built in 1901 for *The Daily Record* newspaper.

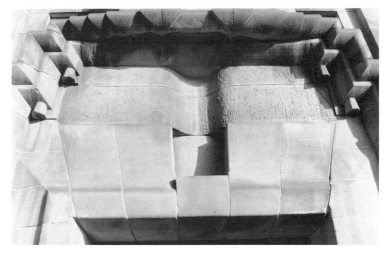

of Mackintosh's commercial buildings. The entrances to *The Daily Record* offices of 1901 combine gigantic over-emphasis with protruding door frames; here the hugely enlarged keystone was originally to have been carved (illus. 43). High above, almost invisible from the narrow lane, the cornice of the building is in richly modelled red sandstone.

In effect, Mackintosh uses detailed stonework to confirm or deny the overall balances and imbalances of his architectural compositions. The result is to create unexpected effects from the most intractable of materials: we can never tell, as we turn the corner of a Mackintosh building, what will come next. This is especially so with the School of Art, since each of the east, north and west stone façades is different from the last, and we pass from neo-vernacular to Glasgow Style to proto-modernism by turning two corners. The effect is the more remarkable because we never think of the School as being anything other than a unified composition.

The south-facing elevation – which is quite definitely a 'back' – is rendered with the rough painted cement known in Scotland as 'harling'. In this respect Mackintosh followed local practice: the technique is perfectly suited to the wet and windy conditions of the region, and even the great terraces built by Alexander Thomson are harled at the rear. Though Mackintosh was financially constrained when building the School, he clearly did not despise harling: for both Hill House and Windyhill, Mackintosh's finest dwellings, he employed this most traditional finishing with a great sensitivity, and it acts as a unifying skin that tightens the visual complexity of the elevations. Harling makes all these buildings seem more traditional than they are, and it gives the complicated 'back' of the School an overall consistency it might otherwise lack.

Mackintosh's stonework contains a strong element of play and pure pleasure; but it also implies particular attitudes to history and modernity on the part of the designer. It affirms, in the overall forms and methods, the local and 'natural' qualities of the vernacular while setting them to generate originality; thus the treatment of stone becomes a kind of high-wire tension between two extremes. What largely vanishes are the historical precedents that, for most of the nineteenth century, had constituted the 'styles'. Mackintosh's stonework is a public proclamation of modernity; but a modernity based upon local conditions and practices.

The material and the structural are difficult topics to separate when speaking of any existing building or interior, since we do not see any materials that are not joined in some way. It is at the point where two members or planes join that the character of material is most revealed. But this point of revelation is, as it were, doubly revealing, for it declares both the material *and* the structural reasons for the joint. I use the word 'declare' because there is a declamatory quality to the emphasis Mackintosh gives the meeting-points between the parts of a building or a piece of furniture: the structure draws attention to itself. Nowhere is this more clearly seen than in the halls, stairways and other spaces that mediate between public and private.

An early example will clarify this assertion. In the main hall of the Martyr's Public School, each of the descending rafters comes to rest on its own little post, which in turn is held between two corbel-shaped brackets; pegs pass through both posts and brackets and protrude on either side, quite prominently. The pegs are sufficiently visible to form a line of visual accents, thus: = = = = = =. The brackets are at the level of the joists in the next space and appear to be formed by the progression of those joists through the wall. Thus the timbers of the main hall seem to be one structure with those of the stairwells and classrooms. Most photographs convey something of this, and it is the effect that was clearly intended: we are encouraged to experience the roof timbers as a continuously connected system, not unlike a complicated umbrella, extending over the stairwells, the rooms and the central hall, with each part pegged to the next. At each outer wall of the stairs the system comes to rest on very solid beams, which on the inside function as corbels that support twinned posts, but which on the outside appear as massive rafters. The eye can follow the lines of the different load-bearing members and comprehend the forces involved, while at the same time the structure can be imagined being folded up or, perhaps, even coming apart like a wooden toy (illus. 44). But the visual impression is deceiving, for the rafters in the stairwell are single, while recent renovations have revealed that the lines of brackets are made from little noggins of wood nailed into a tangle of woodwork that would normally be hidden. The

44 Cross-section sketch by the author to show the roof-truss timbers with their pegged joints as designed by Mackintosh for the Martyr's Public School, Glasgow (1895-6).

45 Mackintosh's timber brackets in the rafters of the Martyr's Public School.

brackets are a theatrical device: they perform no mechanical work at all. They are not, as they appear to be, the continuation of the joists from the stairwell (illus. 45). A similar device can be seen over the altar in the Queen's Cross Church: a single, notional, rafter is clasped between two verticals, which clasp the real rafter above.

When designing and building the Martyr's School, Mackintosh was under numerous constraints and not fully responsible for its design; too much should not be made of this example. But the building reveals something of the young man's aesthetic priorities and provides a general guide to our understanding of the artistic character of his structures, which

46 View across and above Mackintosh's stairwell in the Martyr's Public School, showing the hanging-posts, the beams and the six corbels, which appear externally as beams.

we have already seen to some degree in the stonework: his principal intention is not to express the structure, but to give us the experience of structuring. Take, for example, the trusses over the stairwells: these, technically, are queen-post trusses, but the vertical members appear to hang down and clasp the lower horizontal joists rather than stand on them and support those above. The point of contact is emphasized by three prominent pegs and by a decorative heart motif. The real mechanical work is being done by the large beams that go across the space and which are supported on sturdy stone corbels (illus. 46). At the outer wall the joists are 'supported' from below by six paired hanging posts that stand astride the corbels and clasp the rafters above (illus. 47). The corbels themselves, passing right through the wall, appear from outside the building as beams that indicate the ceiling height inside, and suggest a construction that is far more massive and traditional in character. This rugged exterior is contradicted by the delicacy of the timbering within.

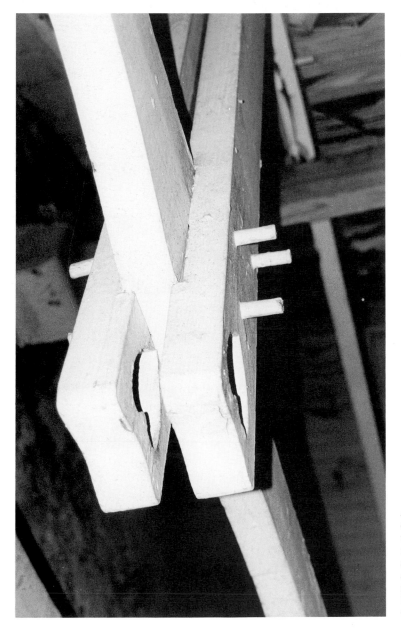

47 Mackintosh's queen-posts – which are not really posts at all – among the timbers above the stairwell in the Martyr's Public School, Glasgow (1895-6).

48 View from the north-east of the Martyr's Public School, showing (beneath the slates) the large beams that, on the inside, form the corbels on which the roof-trusses appear to be supported.

49 A run of Mackintosh's concrete brackets beneath a flight of stairs in the Martyr's Public School.

Prominent and specially shaped corbels are a feature of the Martyr's School: they appear in the stairwell, and in the main hall supporting the massive trusses over the 'atrium'. There is also a run of shapely concrete brackets beneath each flight of stairs that provide yet another line of visual accents (illus. 49).

The use of clearly visible pegged joints was a commonplace of neo-vernacular timberwork to the point of tedium. It was a deliberate and signifying device employed by numerous designers. But here at the Martyr's School it does not signify 'the traditional', but suggests the demountability of the structure. If we imagine these designs translated into contemporary engineering, we find ourselves in a similar aesthetic realm to that of 'high-tech' building, in which the joints and braces of the structure are the primary visual accents, and which are frequently designed with the greatest possible finesse in order not only to bring out their mechanical function but associations of ideas and emotional empathy as well. The 'expression' of construction is taken to the point of 'ex-

pressionism' in these designs; and it is not structure that is being 'honestly' expressed, but the metaphors of clasping, securing, loosing and dismantling. Thus the method of construction becomes a means for creating metaphors and complex associations.

The treatment of timberwork in this early building feeds into all the subsequent designs in unpainted wood. The use of twinned members – such a notable feature of the Martyr's School – becomes most dramatic over the stairwells of the Scotland Street School (1904–6), but many other instances exist, both in buildings and furniture. In the Composition Room of the School of Art, the roof-truss is entirely composed of such timbers, clustering around two posts to form a 'tree'; this motif (and there can be constructional as well as decorative motifs) is repeated in the legs and struts of the drawing desks. As I noted earlier, the same method of construction appears in a table for Hous'hill, Nitshill, Glasgow (Hous'hill was demolished in 1933 after a fire), which Billcliffe describes as 'miniaturizing some of the elements of the Library

50 Detail of a mahogany table of 1910 designed by Mackintosh. Hunterian Art Gallery, University of Glasgow, Mackintosh Collection.

timbers'.[68] The most beautiful of all these structures, per- haps, is the exquisite mahogany table, dated by Billcliffe to 1910, in the Hunterian Art Gallery (illus. 50). Here, the designer combined twinned beams, the 'crossbow' construc- tion and the four-square 'lattice' in a kind of summation and farewell.

The use of pegged twin struts is the simplest method of construction available to the carpenter, and, to some degree, Mackintosh took what was a standard practice and aes- theticized it. It is frequently found in those roof-trusses that are normally hidden from view; it also has something in common with children's constructional toys, in that it can be taken apart as easily as it can be assembled. Thus the sense of security engendered by knowing how a building is con- structed is balanced by the knowledge that it can be taken to pieces; construction is set against de-construction, producing a nervous intensity. The movements toward integration and disintegration are also present. In all this there is an element of ambivalence and poised excitement, for which the term 'fetishization' is, perhaps, entirely appropriate.

Another instance in which construction draws attention to itself is to be found in the long series of designs based around squares and cubes; these are all summarized in the famous square table for Hill House (illus. 51). This is a fantasia upon the relations between three and four and between square and cube, in which it is impossible to distinguish between structure and decoration; to the contemporary eye it is less a forerunner of modern design than it is a piece of conceptual

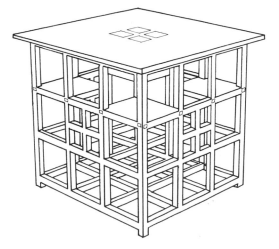

51 Drawing by J. Paterson showing a table designed by Mackintosh in 1902 for Hill House, Helensburgh.

sculpture that is itself and alludes to itself simultaneously. In this case, of course, the actual jointing is disguised under an ebonized finish, and we are left with an object that is as much an idea as a thing.

52 The Library designed and built by Mackintosh in 1907-9 for the Glasgow School of Art.

The most complete example in which all these devices and strategies come together is the Library of the School of Art (1907–9). The emotional intensity of this interior space is generated by the tension between its self-evident integration and the equally evident fact of its assembly from many demountable elements (illus. 52).

On entering the Library, either from below or through the upper door, we are confronted with an array of components immaculately notched and locked into one another, but which are all clearly separate entities: there are both large components, the pillars and twinned joists, and smaller pieces, such as the ingenious side panels of the reading desks. The pillars are assembled out of smooth planks, each one of which has a separate mechanical function. The illumination in the room, which at first seems to be low, brings out the principle of fabrication by picking out the distinctions between parts; in so doing it releases a decorative shimmer. The smooth woodwork contrasts with the rough-sawn plank-work in the corridor outside and emphasizes the special nature of the Library. The main members have clearly been cut and planed by machinery, but their rectilinearity is relieved by the carved details and the undulating balcony rail. All the parts are held to be distinct from one another, and we can well imagine that it was fabricated elsewhere and brought in for final assembly only at the last moment. This impression is strengthened when we realize that the windows and light-wells are independent of the structure of the room itself, and are, in fact, functions of the massive walls; and it is confirmed when we discover that the ceiling of the Library is, in actuality, suspended from the ceiling of the room above by wrought-iron hangers. The timber cage of the Library is then experienced as having been delicately inserted into the masonry container of the west wing, like a stage set suspended from the fly-tower of a theatre. There is nothing quite like this mixture of delicate ingenuity with monumental power; the Library is one of those rooms that causes one to feel with Eliphaz the Temanite, that 'a spirit passed before my face; the hair of my flesh stood up'.

90

But the task of designing, constructing and assembling this room on site (while the building was still functioning as a school) was a task greatly facilitated by Mackintosh's experience as a shopfitter and humble converter of given spaces; and, presumably, by the experience of the building team (which may well have included shipfitting, where such problems are routine). The timberwork fits together, once again, like a kit of parts, each part having been produced separately; and it is not solely the components that are separate, but the tasks of making them. This is an ensemble made with, and exploiting the possibilities of, a fully mechanical workshop. The nature of the workmanship is such that the qualities of the materials are subordinated to the design process. Mackintosh's allegiances, as they appear in his lectures of 1892–3 and from what we know about his working practice (frequently remodelling the design in the process of building), place him and his early work within the traditions of the Arts and Crafts Movement.[69] As late as 1902, in the lecture notes entitled 'Seemliness', he was still referring to the 'art-worker' and the 'architect as artist'. But the character of the Library and of similar spaces, such as the staircase at Hill House, shows how far his actual practice had moved away from his early stated convictions.

To demonstrate the originality of the Library and its unique cultural significance in the British Isles, we can usefully compare it to a similar building designed by the English architect and furniture designer Ernest Gimson (1864–1920). The Library of Gimson's Bedales School, Hampshire (illus. 53), was designed in 1919 and completed two years later; it is part of a sturdy building in brick and masonry modelled on the traditional barn structures that Gimson had studied in great detail and which he admired for their rustic nobility. His Library employs massive timber-posts and trusses, with exposed rafters and joints. The contrast between the interiors of these two libraries can be followed down into small details of workmanship – the differing use of pegged joints, the tapering and chamfering of both main and subsidiary members, the use of tools (adzes and spokeshaves, as against rotary planes and mechanical saws). This contrast can be described in Geddesian terms as one between the palaeotechnic and the neotechnic; but Gimson's preference for the older mode was not forced upon him by necessity; comparing the

53 The Library,
Bedales School,
Hampshire
(1919-21), by Ernest
Gimson.

two sorts of workmanship reveals a fundamental difference in orientation. Gimson's design grows out of the neo-vernacular doctrines of the Arts and Crafts Movement; his interior is fixated upon a studiously researched ideal prototype. The philosophical foundations and ideological impetus that inform the Bedales Library are exactly those that led Gimson's colleagues to condemn the Glasgow Style as 'distinctly unhealthy and revolting'. Seen from the Scots and European perspectives, however, the Bedales Library represents the end of a development and the rigidity of a clientele that had once seemed revolutionary. It is the dead end of a localism that has rejected modernity. Mackintosh, on the other hand, successfully attempted the difficult feat of using machined finishes and prefabrication to achieve a highly individual artistic effect.

I argued before that Mackintosh's decoration was informed by Symbolist painting; and that his attitude to materials and their structuring was influenced by W. R. Lethaby's *Architecture, Mysticism and Myth* (1892), which brought into the world of architecture something of the imaginative richness of Symbolist thinking. Lethaby conceived a building to be an image of the cosmos, in which the pillars and the roof-trees are the Tree of Life upholding the Vault of Heaven. Lethaby's symbolism – in which the archaic and the modernist are inextricably mixed – was without doubt part of the overall mental formation of the young Mackintosh.[70] In a revised edition of *Architecture, Mysticism and Myth* Lethaby noted that its main thesis was 'that the development of building practice and ideas of the world structure acted and reacted on one another', and the 'magical properties generally had a very wide and deep influence on the development of ancient building customs'. Seen from this Symbolist perspective, the fetishization of structure suggests an insecurity overcome by a dynamic and deliberate Will. I think there is little doubt that in this there is a psychobiographical element; but this element is much less interesting than the broader cultural condition it expresses. That cultural condition is the collapse of the accepted system of historical precedence and the anxiety this collapse induced.

There is another task Mackintosh gave to carpentry: that of providing spatial clues which are subtly at variance with reality. True always to his vernacular point of departure, Mackintosh did his best to avoid the pure column, while happily employing timber posts. The problem of 'termination' was resolved in a very simple way by using a flat plate or wide moulding, a device he had evidently borrowed from A. H. Mackmurdo. Three examples illustrate the uses to which these terminations were put (illus. 54, 55 and 56). In none of these examples are we dealing with genuine, mechanically necessary, means of support. Though these extended newel-posts steady their banisters, the plates in which they terminate are rhetorical devices. What they support are volumes – either filled space (mass) or void. In none of these examples is any serious weight involved. In the Museum Room of the School of Art, the plates in which the tall mast-like posts end, both mark and create the visual distinction between the room space and the ceiling space. Furthermore, in some cases in the School of Art, and possibly elsewhere, posts that appear to be made of wood are in fact made of steel. They are doing mechanical work, to be sure, but not that which they appear to be doing. This is a further instance of Mackintosh's theatricality. Generally, Mackintosh used

54 Newel-post and plate by Mackintosh at the top of a flight of stairs in Queen's Cross Church, Glasgow (1898-9).

Mackintosh was to repeat the simple square plate shown here in Hill House, Helensburgh (1902-3), where the square also serves to reinforce the fourfold modulation of furniture and decoration.

55 Close-up of one of Mackintosh's newel-posts in Queen's Cross Church.

This square section post is sensitively chamfered down so that the eye passes easily from straight to curve.

56 Pillar supporting a beam in Mackintosh's Queen's Cross Church.

This plate gives a powerful horizontal accent and makes no pretence to be part of the 'support'. Similar features are to be found in the School of Art's Museum.

wooden mouldings and other woodwork details to create the experience of space rather than to mark out real spatial boundaries. Space is being defined both psychologically and metrically; and the two forms of definition are being played off against one another.

Indeed, the artistic function of Mackintosh's use of carpentry in these situations is to play with our experience of space and structure, by forcing us to pay an ambivalent attention to both. I would describe this as a phenomenological approach to the architectural interior. Mackintosh makes a distinction between the world as measured and the world as experienced, and neither fits exactly onto the other. Both are present, but we can only see one at a time. Significantly, this ambivalence, or equivocation, comes into play in the intermediate zone between inner and outer, between the private and the public domains.

Metals, wrought-iron in particular, make up the material that most preserves Mackintosh's submerged graphic fantasia; metals carry linear invention straight from the sketch-pad to the building. Obvious examples of this are to be seen in the crests that run across the front of the School of Art, in the rose-knots that terminate its window brackets, and in the leaded lights. Less obvious are the strip-work grilles that enclose the stair-heads and which, in taking up the rectangular and circular motifs that pass thoughout the building, stand for the geometric principles of the drawing-board and look forward to the table at Hill House, while at the same time making Gothick associations with castle architecture (illus. 57). A similar device is found at the top of the stairs in Scot-

57 Stair-head iron grille designed by Mackintosh in 1896-8 during the first phase of the Glasgow School of Art.

58 Detail of
decorative
wrought-ironwork
by Mackintosh for
Queen's Cross
Church, Glasgow
(1898-9).

land Street School, where a large iron circle, or hoop, alludes
to the cylindricality of the stair-tower. Iron is also the medium
through which the naturalistic motifs and allusions – emblematic birds and leaves – were brought into the School of Art.
Generally speaking, iron is the medium that is used pic-
torially, in that the prototypes of the forms it takes can most
easily be traced back to graphic imagery; it illustrates the
origins of the whole design and summarizes the decorative
principles. There is also at least one instance in which ironwork can be seen to be setting forth its own craft: in the
railings of Queen's Cross Church there is a form that, reminiscent of the 'head' of the immured figure in *The Tree of
Influence*, emblemizes the blacksmith's tongs (illus. 58). Here
it is as if the iron has become conscious of itself as having
been wrought. Ironwork becomes the bearer of wit; it is the
most playful and self-allusive element.

Steel, on the other hand, is business-like. It was just at the
moment when Mackintosh was moving towards his mature
work that the use of steel frames for construction was becoming common practice. Glasgow, once filled with steelworkers
and boilermakers, contains some of the first structures of this

59 Bolted steel
joists in
Mackintosh's
Scotland Street
School, Glasgow
(1904-6).

kind. Mackintosh used steel beams sparingly, and he made no attempt to hide them in concrete or masonry, although, as we have seen, he was not above passing steel off as wood. The use of steel beams in the School of Art has often been commented on, but they also appear, frankly displayed, in the Martyr's School and play an important part in the Scotland Street School, where they are used to support the stairs (illus. 59).

Mackintosh's light-fittings are a subject in themselves. He was, of course, working at a time when electrical devices and modern service systems had not yet been standardized, and when a number of new plastic materials were becoming available. We can see how he struggled to find shapes that were both effective and harmonious with the overall design. The hanging lamps in the Library of the School of Art, or the large hall and stairwell lamps in Hill House, are successful as shapes, but as dispensers of light they are, perhaps, less than perfect. These lamps were cut and bent – as if from paper – from thin brass or zinc, and they mimic the forms of the buildings in which they are found.[71]

Brackets, pegs, door furniture and other details are rarely standardized, and Mackintosh's metal window-frames appear to have been made to his own specification. In this domain we are closest to that world of the shipfitter discussed in Chapter 1; we are dealing with a realm whose objects and processes are not easily categorized. Firms such as Wylie & Lochead were among the first to sell electric lamps, so there was, evidently, a growing knowledge of what might be required for this new amenity. I suspect, but cannot demonstrate, that in electrical and other advanced technology, Mackintosh was drawing upon experience gained by those who worked in the fitting-out trades. Hill House, for example, contains a remarkable shower, the horizontal jets of which spurt from a series of chromed copper pipes arranged in a sort of cage; this looks as though its origins are maritime.

COLOUR: GLASS, CERAMICS AND ENAMEL

In Mackintosh's work, glass, ceramic and enamel have a small but important role to play: they are the principal means by which bright colour enters a building. Accents of colour are used throughout his public buildings as way-markers and insignia; the coloured tiles on the stairwells of the School of Art, for example, had been invoked two years earlier in the atrium of the Martyr's School. Several doors in the School of Art have small leaded lights with emblematic designs – seeds, birds, roses – that take up the themes and functions of the metalwork. Particularly important here is the female emblem at the entrance doors. This tree/woman, who clasps a scarlet rose at a place that has been daintily described as 'halfway between her head and her feet',[72] denotes that this is a building presided over by the female principle.

In Mackintosh's private houses these little panes of coloured glass have a more abstract function, bringing a note of expectancy into dark interiors. Particularly good examples of this can be found in Hill House, where the doors have small patches of glowing colour set in them; as you enter a room you pass from the dark hall by way of these entrances, which the colours have endowed with an atmosphere of anticipation. As for the bedroom furniture at Hill House, there are patches of bright enamel at the bed-foot and bright, pinkish tiles give an emphasis to the alcoves. The purpose of these touches of colour is, as we shall see, important for the iconography of the white, private interiors.

Having studied the manner in which Mackintosh displayed the materials and the structure of his designs, we must now look at those instances in which the opposite principles govern. To do so we must turn from the most public rooms – halls, libraries, museums and churches – by way of offices and living rooms to the most private – the bedrooms; and in so doing we pass from the most rugged surfaces to the most smooth. The associations are quite clear: we turn from the masculine realm, with its declamation of structure, to feminine interiority and silkiness. The distinction I am making here is, of course, highly conventionalized and part of the ideology of gender that was firmly rooted in nineteenth-century assumptions. What I hope to show is that Mackintosh, while maintaining the rhetoric of masculine/feminine associations, pushed them beyond the conventions within which they were conceived.

In moving so directly to the most private, my intention is to dramatize the differences. Between the two extremes are several intermediate stages – the offices, studies, entrance hall and tea-rooms in which a modified privacy and public space intermingle. The treatment of these spaces and rooms is appropriate to the rhetoric; thus the different parts of the tea-rooms are treated in different ways, while the offices and boardroom of the School of Art (and the study at Hill House) are 'masculine', but delicately so. (The boardroom of the School of Art is 'masculine', but it is a masculinity that is subverted by humour.) Domestic interiors (including the Mackintoshes' Mains Street apartment) follow this general rule. Entrance halls and dining-rooms are generally dark, with exposed carpentry and 'real' materials; disguised materials increasingly appear the more private the space is.

The white interiors also form the realm for which the collaboration with Margaret Macdonald becomes an issue of some importance. The view taken here is that the white interiors (most importantly, the Mackintoshes' own Mains Street apartment, now preserved in the Hunterian Art Gallery in Glasgow) were created by Mackintosh and Macdonald working together. By this I do not mean that the actual design work was always equally shared, but that the overall concepts that guided the designs were the product of a shared imagination. If the rooms of the apartment on Mains Street are taken as the type for all the other white interiors, then this notion of

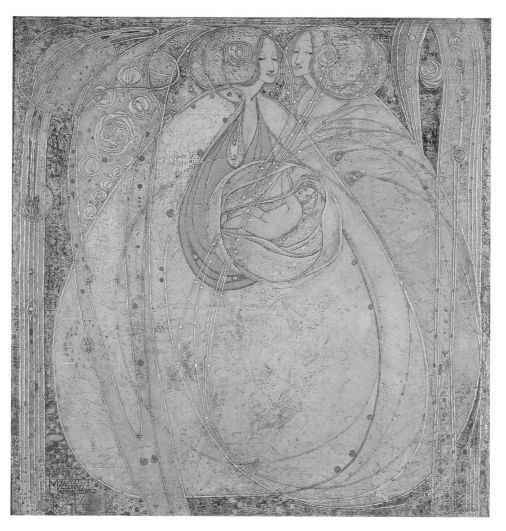

60 Margaret Mackintosh, *The Heart of the Rose*, one of a pair of painted gesso panels made for the Turin Exhibition of 1902. Glasgow School of Art.

61 Mirror
designed by
Mackintosh in 1901
for his apartment in
Mains Street.
Hunterian Art
Gallery, University
of Glasgow,
Mackintosh
Collection.

a shared imagination should be accepted, since it is difficult to imagine two such creative and close individuals not working together on their own private space. The poetic system ought to be perceived as the product of two minds, a perception that substantially enlarges our understanding of Macdonald's work.

The character of the white interiors is not wholly unique; there are many examples of more or less open eroticism in the private spaces of the Aesthetic Movement and in Art Nouveau boudoirs. What makes the white interiors so striking, however, is that they are all located within buildings that are, externally, fairly sober, and they are reached by halls and stairways that exemplify expressed construction. Just as the drawings and paintings of the Macdonald sisters were more metamorphic, and more original, in their imagery than other and greater artists among the Symbolists, so there is nothing that fully prepares us for the shock we experience when we first encounter these rooms – a shock that closer acquaintance does not diminish.[73] This, in large measure, is due to the qualities of workmanship. A notable feature is the absence of any obvious trace of the workman's hand. All large surfaces are meticulously crafted to a uniform sleekness, and to such a degree that in low levels of light the exact location of the surface is not readily apparent to the eye. This is the very opposite of the rugged treatment of stone and the self-conscious joinery that is such a feature of more public spaces and surfaces. Three examples will suffice (illus. 62, 63 and 64).

The effect of these surfaces is not wholly visual; indeed, the eye is partly deceived by them and we look for security in the sense of touch. These objects actually invite touch in the way that the human body does; this is especially true with curved details – those of tables and shelves, for example, and of some cupboard handles. I have written elsewhere of this, with particular reference to the splendid cheval mirror that has pride of place in the restored bedroom now in the Hunterian Art Gallery (illus. 61).[74] The overall effect of the white rooms is to induce a restrained, almost ritualized, sensuousness in those who enter them; behaviour becomes charged with body consciousness.

It is probable that these surfaces were inspired by Japanese lacquerwork; but Glasgow's craftsmen did not have the same skills, and it is only through careful treatment that any of the

62 Detail of the foot of a bed designed by Mackintosh in 1901. Hunterian Art Gallery, University of Glasgow, Mackintosh Collection.

63 Detail of a cupboard designed by Mackintosh in 1901. Hunterian Art
Gallery, University of Glasgow, Mackintosh Collection.

64 Small table designed by Mackintosh in 1901. Hunterian Art Gallery,
University of Glasgow, Mackintosh Collection.

white furniture has survived. They are designs that are far more robustly realized in modern reproductions than they were originally; and today they might well be made in some other material altogether. The small table (illus. 64) is a hidden cousin of those sturdy tables in oak designed for the tea-rooms and similar settings; in this private context it appears like a fantasy version of its public reality. Not only is the material and the method of carpentry obscured, the white surface serves to unify the entire object, both within itself and within the ensemble. By these means the distinctions between objects are reduced in favour of the unity of the whole room. Contrary to established conventions, applied colour becomes a component that has equal importance with form and structure, and this too is part of the poetic pattern. Stone-work was left in its natural colour; timberwork was almost always stained a uniform brown or green; but in these intimate interiors almost nothing has its 'natural' surface or colour. Whereas in the larger public spaces of the School of Art or the Martyr's Public School the colour accents are in strong reds or blues, the more private the space the more the colours become secondary or tertiary hues.[75]

What is termed 'white' is, in fact, an ivory tint (though to what degree this is due to ageing is not clear, and different rooms and items are of slightly different intensities of white). These colour ranges are always in the strongest contrast to those obtaining in the halls and passages, where dark stains, strong hues and natural surfaces are usual, and where lighting is often rich and dim. Typically, a white interior is set off by large areas of grey-brown or fawn carpeting, with touches of deep pink enamel, pale green stencil patterns and the occasional shot of deep red or purple, or mother-of-pearl. Textiles are often undyed and neutral, and the natural colours of hard materials appear only at very particular points – such as the stone surrounding a grate, or the fire-irons. In the bedrooms, these qualities become still more marked. There the range of applied colour corresponds to that of an idealized nudity; both in its hues and in the relation of large areas to small touches.[76] These touches of colour are frequently on the inner surfaces of motifs, as if the whiteness had been opened to uncover the colour within. The sleek finish of the surfaces and the relation of roughness to smoothness, of decorative detail to plain surface, of small forms to large forms,

107

and of angularity to entasis, all speak the language of a diffused and delicate eroticism. This nudity can be interpreted, conventionally, as 'feminine', but an alternative interpretation may suggest the experience of the maternal body: the sensations are of a delicate, perhaps weightless, all-encompassing embrace. The overall colour scheme, which tends to reduce the clear distinctions between objects and to shed a uniform light throughout the space, reinforces this diffusion of feeling and attention. At the heart of this system of poetics there is an undifferentiated tenderness.

There are the mirrors too. Mackintosh designed several large, full-length mirrors, of which the most imposing is the one he designed for the Mains Street bedroom (illus. 61). To stand before this mirror is a curious experience, since the forward, balanced, curve of its frame is that of the female hip and pelvic girdle thrust out very slightly towards one. A man standing before this piece sees himself enclosed in an unmistakably female space; a woman sees not simply herself, but her own contingent figure gathered into the transcendent Feminine. This effect is not brought about solely by the shape of the mirror, but by the thick white lacquer of its surface, which, as Billcliffe remarks, 'suggests some softer, more malleable material underneath'.[77] A mirror is indeed an appropriate object in which to embody and promote a certain quality of privacy, because it contains the possibility of both representation and of emptiness. Before a mirror we become our own spectacle; and just as the white interiors reflect an all-surrounding idealized nudity, so the mirror, solipsistically, throws that reflection back on itself. Moreover, the self that enters a mirror – like the self in fantasy – is without continuity, and vanishes as soon as the beholder looks away; yet, when present, is fascinating. It is a self without social obligation.[78]

Beyond its obvious sexual connotations, what does this sleek workmanship and erotic imagery signify? That an advanced style may be an erotic style is not surprising: Eros liberates the imagination for both good and ill. Many examples could be cited, but a relevant one would be the 'feminisation' of Rococo boudoirs and their furniture, which body forth an involved form of coquetry. Likewise, there is a consistent and modish sexuality evident throughout the diverse phenomena of Art Nouveau and Jugendstil. This sexuality can be powerful (Klimt), mocking (Beardsley) or frivolous (Mucha), or, as in French and Belgian Symbolism, it can be exotic or mystical. Numerous writers have seen in this a disturbance of conventional relations between the sexes, and described it in terms of a 'fin-de-siècle' and the ending of nineteenth-century mores. The eroticism of, for example, Klimt's paintings, is always considered to be laden with male foreboding.

Mackintosh, and the artists who developed the Glasgow Style, partook of this climate of feeling; but in the case of the white interiors a different interpretation yields a richer and more emancipatory vision. The eroticism of Mackintosh is not one that is predicated upon patriarchal anxiety, but one that is embracing and 'oceanic' in its associations. Though his rooms are tense, they do not bleakly threaten. The tension arises from the anxiety that something may occur that will shatter a moment of blissful balance. I suggest that this erotic/maternal atmosphere embodies psychic experiences grounded very early in life, when the lack of differentiation permits and promotes the growth of fantasy. At the psychic level this tenderness is not clearly gendered, nor is it clearly attached to external objects, since they have not yet been firmly identified; rather, the distinction between internal and external worlds is fluid, and still in the process of determination.

A number of writers have seen the source of creative imagination in this early process of differentiation. In achiev-ing a balance between infantile fantasy and the demands of reality we do not opt for one or the other, but resolve the conflict through an imaginative dialectic that, on the one hand frees us from illusion, and on the other from captivity to a meaningless objectification.[79] Early, undifferentiated, con-sciousness precedes learned definitions of reality; it is, there-fore, the ground from which originality and redefinition grows. The white interiors represent a plunge into this heart of innovation from which, in retracing the journey from pri-vate to public, we are able freely to redefine the demands of the objective domain in such a way as to restructure our reality. This plunge and re-emergence is enacted allegorically in the poetics of workmanship.

There is a considerable step from this description of psychic experience to the very practical business of designing and building a house; and I do not wish to present a psychoana-lytic argument that is reductive. But once Mackintosh has been explained in terms of both symbolism and Symbolism, we have to ask – 'symbolic of what?' The system of poetic spaces that encloses these most intimate rooms was organized according to established ninteenth-century gender associations; but these associations were undermined by the reconstruction of reality that has followed from our re-emergence from the system. The 'feminine' that is remade is not domestic, but innovatory and fantastic; thus the poetics of workmanship further enact a redefinition of gender in which the 'feminine' is neither persecutory nor subservient, but, in fact, the forge of modernity. It is created from, and creates, an interior from which all traces of the local vernacular and the historical have either been expelled or utterly transformed.

At the level of design practice, this feat could only be achieved by someone who was capable of absorbing and distilling a quite exceptional range of artistic material, and who had evolved a method of work that enabled this material to be creatively unfolded. This unfolding required an imaginative leap beyond the paradigms of historicism and the neo-vernacular; that is to say, beyond the given context of architecture and design.

Mackintosh's poetics, therefore, imply a reformed conception of humanity: one in which the attainment of modernity is dependent on a change in the relations between the sexes, in which the 'feminine' is the site of innovation. Once this point is established, interpretation can pass from the objects and spaces to the realm of the social, and to ideas about the reform of social life and sexual manners then current. Once again, the writings and activities of Patrick Geddes seem to be important, though the direct points of contact between Mackintosh, Macdonald and Geddes remain obscure. Geddes's *The Evolution of Sex* (1889), co-written with J. A. Thompson, is a critical summary of contemporary biological theory, in which the male and the female are distinguished on the basis of metabolic patterns. Geddes and Thompson were not simply concerned with 'straight' biology: the latter part of their book is taken up with a discussion of 'psychological and ethical aspects'. The authors argued that since there are natural metabolic distinctions between male and female, 'what was decided among the prehistoric Protozoa cannot be annulled by Act of Parliament'. They were sceptical of a merely political feminism that would plunge women into 'the competitive industrial struggle', and, equally, of a simple-minded 'biologism' in which 'the past of the race is depicted in the most sinister colours. . . . [The] absolute ratification of this by law and religion was merely of a piece with the whole order of belief and practice, in which men crushed themselves still more than their mates'. For them, the task facing society in 1889 was the 'reconstitution of that complex and sympathetic co-operation between the differentiated sexes in and around which all progress, past or future, must depend . . . the social order will clear itself as it comes more in touch with biology'.[80] What follows is a discussion of contraception and a final vision (augmented with a spiral diagram) whereby 'the ideal before us is a more harmonious blending of the two streams'.

The Evolution of Sex made a strong impression on many young Scots; one wrote that 'In the 1890s multitudes of young men in Scotland and in England owed their souls to the teachings of Patrick Geddes'.[81] There seems to be little doubt that it was read in the School of Art, since we find that in 1900 Francis Newbery wrote and produced a masque entitled 'The (R)evolution of Women'.[82]

If my interpretation of this poetics is correct, then we need to think of the Mackintosh / Macdonald white rooms, and their relation to the intermediate and exterior spaces of his architecture, as being a significant statement about gender. I have suggested before that, in today's terms, the equation of femininity with interiority is not fully emancipatory; but in Geddes's terms it is: *The Evolution of Sex* implies an ideology of 'equal but different' that sanctions, indeed encourages, a significant cultural difference between the sexes, based upon fundamental metabolism. Geddes portrayed existing cultural traditions as sinister and crushing, in which to be invited to participate in equal opportunity was merely to be drawn into a 'gladiator's show'; Geddes's argument could be extended to assert the necessity of distinct female cultural institutions. We cannot now know the degree to which these ideas, and others related to them, went to form the spaces I have been describing; but it seems unmistakable to me that the closer one goes to the centre of the system, the more the feminine becomes identified with the unprecedented. And this seems to be the meaning of a poetics of workmanship that attempts at once to synthesize vernacular and modern, male and female and outer and inner.

4 Modernity and the Interior

The question that has been emerging in the course of this book – the nature of Mackintosh's modernity – must now be confronted. Glasgow has been identified as an aggressively modern city, in which the most advanced and colossal technology existed side by side with an eclectic architectural tradition and an adventurous artistic life. Mackintosh's education embodied the cultural stresses and contradictions of his background, and his means for resolving and synthesizing these problems were, essentially, graphic: the methods of drawing he developed were the means by which a unity of imagery and feeling could be created from many disparate elements. This imagery, to be fully integrated into the fabric of the building, had to be realized through a poetics of workmanship that bodied forth the poles of this experience and enacted the tensions between them. This was a remarkable feat of practical and imaginative intelligence, for which there was a price to be paid: 'Shake off all the props – the props tradition and authority offer you – and go alone – crawl – stumble – stagger – but go alone – You cannot learn to walk without tumbles and knocks and bruises, but you will never learn to walk so long as there are props'.[83] But the aim was the attainment of a modern style that would signal a general reform of life toward the goal of 'sweetness, simplicity, freedom, confidence and light'.[84]

Hermann Muthesius brought out very clearly the transcendental and 'impractical' element in Mackintosh's designs for the white interiors, and we are reminded of Mackintosh's notes on 'things more beautiful, more precious, more lasting than life.' Muthesius saw these rooms as the prophetic extension of the Aesthetic Movement:

Once the interior attains the status of a work of art, that is, when it is intended to embody aesthetic values, the artistic effect must obviously be heightened to the utmost. The Mackintosh group does this and no-one will reproach them on this particular point. Whether such enhancement is appropriate to our everyday rooms is another question. Mackintosh's rooms are refined to a degree which the lives of even the artistically educated are still a long way from matching. The delicacy and austerity of their artistic atmosphere would tolerate no admixture of the ordinariness which fills our lives. Even a book in an unsuitable binding would disturb the atmosphere simply by lying on the table, indeed even the man or woman of today – especially the man in his unadorned working attire – treads like a stranger in this fairy-tale world. There is for the time being no possibility of our aesthetic cultivation playing so large a part in our lives that rooms like this could be general. But they are milestones placed by a genius far ahead of us to mark the way to excellence for mankind in the future.[85]

Those who have lived in a Mackintosh house attest somewhat differently. They are far more practical than the museum visitor might suppose, full of attention to real needs and ordinary pleasures, while the public buildings have proved very serviceable and are loved by those who have worked in them. But the atmosphere is undeniable – 'highly charged . . . of a mystical, symbolic kind'. The visitor is always impressed by this; and not always favourably, since the all-encompassing unity of the interiors and the way in which they are poetically linked to other rooms – indeed, to the whole construction – demonstrates a total grasp of the environment, a grasp that takes control of our own senses and associations.

The interpretation put forward in these pages thus far has been that through their methods of invention and the poetics of workmanship, these buildings and interiors create a means of access to unconscious fantasy and the sources of innovation. And they do so in a way that links that innovation to an a-temporal regional vernacular, thus 'short-circuiting' the academic tradition. But the journey can be reversed: we can, as it were, retrace our steps outward, from the forge of modernity to the 'natural' and 'pristine' objectivity of the vernacular.

We leave the master bedroom of Hill House (white, deep-pink and smooth) for the upper landing, where an alcove lined in dark stained wood provides a meeting place for children; we descend the splendid, ample cylinder of the

stairwell (illus. 71), with its amazing newel-post and cage of carpentry, passing from the light into the dark and richly coloured hall (illus. 65). Here everything is rectilinear, sharply articulated and emphatic. We pass by the study (a room that is entirely business-like, yet hinting at the subtleties above) and leave through a sturdy but unobtrusive front door. In the small, traditional porch there is a stencilled device (illus. 66) that balances the geometrical with the organic. Once outside, we look back at a house that is thoroughly traditional in its materials, and might be thought almost plain were it not for some extremely precise details. The iron gate (illus. 67) stands as a sign of what we have already found inside. Turning toward the village we feel a cold wind blowing off the Firth of Clyde; it tears the wet leaves off the trees.

Each of the several stages of this journey from master bedroom to main gate has its own highly charged atmosphere. Each stage, each experience, is a necessary element in the complete experience of Hill House, and each needs to be examined if the full meaning of Mackintosh's project is to be brought out.

The master bedroom of Hill House is more sober than the bedroom of the Mains Street apartment, but its formal language is essentially the same. I have already identified this

65 Ceiling and light-fittings in the hallway at Hill House, Helensburgh (1902-3).

In the hallway at Hill House, pink and dark-blue details are set off against brass and dark stained wood.

66 Stencilled
design in the porch
at Hill House,
Helensburgh.

*In this design the
ghost of art botany
floats through the
geometric mesh.*

67 Wrought-iron
gate at Hill House,
Helensburgh.

*Mackintosh used
ironwork for its
graphic and allusive
qualities, and this
gate gives an
indication of what lies
ahead within the
vernacular massing of
Hill House itself.*

kind of space as being, within the terms of the poetics, a feminine space. But what of the roots of this 'femininity'? Where does it fit within the general character of the Arts Nouveaux, all of which were permeated by concepts of femininity that appeared both in reactionary and progressive modes? Indeed, throughout the whole of the *fin de siècle* the emancipatory and the retardaire are linked, in some cases almost inextricably.[86]

The gender aspect of Parisian Art Nouveau has been extensively studied by Deborah Silverman, who finds links between that movement and the ideological struggle within French society between the 'traditional' and the 'new' Woman. This struggle was, in turn, linked to an essentially conservative and nostalgic concept of national identity, consequent upon the débâcle of the Franco-Prussian War of 1870–1 and the socialist uprising of the Commune. In an attempt to recover the lost glories of French tradition, which were designated as decorative rather than scientific and craftsmanlike rather than industrial, Government circles encouraged the growth of the 'new art', identifying it with a 'modern' domesticity that was antagonistic to the undomesticated and autonomous New Woman. The effect was 'to define and promote women as the natural allies of French luxury craftsmen, and as the artificers of a unitary interior design'.[87] This social ideology was supported by a *psychologie nouvelle*, which attributed to women a particular nervous constitution that naturally expressed itself through a heightened sensitivity to line, colour and form. This, in its reactionary mode, may be seen as a reworking in pseudo-scientific terms of much older stereotypes: the medical language of neurasthenia, for example, has much in common with the affective language of Symbolism. But in its progressive mode this new psychology accorded women the special task of innovation. The fashioning of the new interior was, by analogy, a refashioning of the inner life to meet the demands of a new age.

Here we encounter the complicated question of different interpretations of phenomena that seem, on first acquaintance, similar. The enthusiastic reception of the Glasgow Style in Vienna and Budapest is well documented, and the mutual influences involving Glasgow and central Europe have been extensively studied. The Jugendstil represented an attempt to create a style that was independent of conservative nationalism, a style that would denote a scientific modernity.[88] The Glasgow Style, as personified in Mackintosh and Macdonald, seems to have offered a possible model, combining modernity with subjectivity. Silverman convincingly argues a contrary case, that Parisian Art Nouveau was part of a reaction through which 'a cult of the self emerged to compensate for the challenges to individuality wrought by machine production and colossal technology'.[89] This was specifically opposed to the scientistic and Positivist ideology of previous decades. The new art was conceived in terms of a revival of the values of the Rococo, a recovery of the aristocratic manner.

In the case of Mackintosh, this explanation cannot hold. The habitual British compensation for the stresses and challenges of modernity was, and continues to be, the reification of 'character' and a preoccupation with 'tradition'. But Glasgow in 1900 was at the apogee of its power and wealth, and the very centre of massive technology; there is no sign in anything that Mackintosh wrote of any compensation. Nor was there anything in the way of an authentic aristocratic precedent that could be so revived. What, then, are the foundations of this concern with gender and its associations?

I believe three principal sources can be identified, although the first of these I put forward in a spirit of speculation. Alex Owen has recently shown how the Spiritualist Movement was an early contributor to feminism. Spiritualism, in its outward manifestations, depended upon a passive femininity; but it contained a powerful claim for the spiritual superiority of passivity, and it made these claims in the context of a quasi-scientific cosmology. Passivity, in fact, became synonymous with power. Owen describes this situation as 'a crucial departure from its hegemonic meaning, and, in a move which potentially transformed gender categories, men also earnestly sought to develop it'.[90] What Owen barely touches on is the relation of the Movement to a whole realm of iconography, and to the practice of 'automatic' writing and drawing, now well recognized as among the chief sources of twentieth-century art. Of relevance here is the case of Georgina Ward-Houghton, whose 'spirit drawings' of the 1870s have been studied from time to time. One commentator described them thus:

Lines drawn with a marvellous combination of freedom and precision, and in a great variety of colours, depart from ever shifting foci . . . with every variety of curve; they meet and part and intersect each other, incidentally yielding singular contrasts of linear perspective and colour blendings and contrasts. . . .[91]

68 Detail of bed-foot, part of a piece of furniture designed by Mackintosh in 1902 for Hill House, Helensburgh.

69 Detail to be seen in the living-room at Hill House, Helensburgh.

70 Light-fitting in the hallway at Hill House, Helensburgh.

It may be that the methods of drawing and the female iconography of the Glasgow Style stand in a similar relationship to late Spiritualism as, for example, the portraits and full-length studies of women in Mondrian's early work stand to Theosophy.[92] Whatever may be the case, English critics responded uneasily to the 'spook style'. It is not, of course, essential for my argument that there should have been any such direct connection. The Spiritualist movements of the late nineteenth century, in all their varying and sometimes disreputable windings, are yet related in that they were all consequent upon the decay of Positivism, and all in some measure exalt the feminine.

But the cult of the feminine was powerfully reinforced from within the very centre of Positivism, as part of the new 'Religion of Humanity'.[93] This religious humanism was proposed and given a semi-ritual form in order to embody the 'subjective synthesis' by which human consciousness and affections are linked to reality. This stage in mental development recognizes and avows its subjectivity and so makes it available to Positive thought; this makes it superior to primitive, unanalysed subjectivity, which is the source of delusions. Humanity is conceived of as female, as 'She', and Her religion as the outcome of the dialectic that passes from the theological to the metaphysical to be resolved in the Positive. Prayer, in this religion, is addressed to Humanity through an internal, idealized, female figure.[94]

In all this there is a strong element of secularized Mariolatry, and it would be easy to dismiss it as mere crankiness were it not for the pervasive influence of this 'feminism'. The list of those who were in some way touched by it includes J. S. Mill, Harriet Martineau, George Eliot and her circle (which included Owen Jones and A. H. Mackmurdo), numerous contributors to The Westminster Review, and Walter Pater. It was a constant element in the 'progressive' thought of the later half of the century, though by then it had been much refrac-

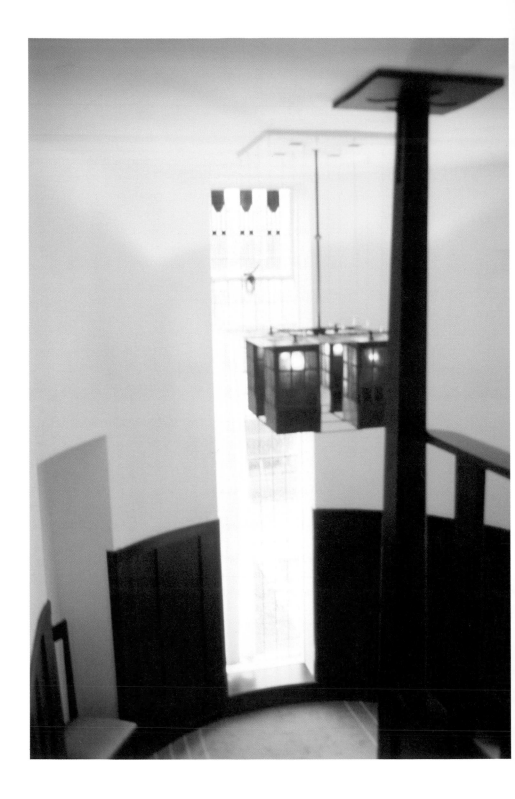

*Four-square
latticework
patterning is found
throughout the
intermediate and
general living-spaces
at Hill House – from
furniture and
light-fittings to
carpets and
carpentry.*

ted. As such, it is a contributory factor to the iconography of
the Aesthetic Movement, which can also be seen as a secularized version of Pre-Raphaelitism; and from thence to Mackintosh and the vision of 'sweetness, simplicity, freedon,
confidence and light'. Indeed, the last figure to have taken
the 'Religion of Humanity' with any literal seriousness was
Patrick Geddes, who in his youth had attended Positivist
sermons in London and whose thinking throughout his life
was permeated with Comtean schema. The now-famous distinction between the 'palaeotechnic' and the 'neotechnic'
epochs, which actually dates from 1898 but was first published in *The Evolution of Cities* in 1915, derives directly from
Comte's categories of civilization. There is little doubt that
the 'feminist' element in Geddes's writings – not least in *The
Evolution of Sex* – is informed by these origins, and that the
drive to synthesize art with science in a new social order
– everywhere apparent in Geddes's work – has a Comtean
foundation. If this argument from the 'Religion of Humanity'
holds good, then we can see that the feminine iconography
of the Glasgow Style is the final stage in the representation
of a major theme in nineteenth-century culture. The fervour
of the Style is, indeed, a religious fervour.

The third source was immediate and local. Under Francis
Newbery the School of Art had become a focus of female
emancipation; the Macdonald sisters and their contemporaries were in the forefront of this movement in Scotland, and
they began their careers with something approaching parity
of esteem with their male peers. In this sense they were 'new
women': acting independently, concerned with professional
advancement, and marrying late. Mackintosh and Margaret
Macdonald worked as a professional partnership on several
occasions, and in Vienna her art was at least as well known
as his. In this respect the Macdonald sisters fit well into a
time of progress and emancipation; the year or so of *The Pond*
and *The Tree of Influence* is the year of George Bernard Shaw's
Candida, while the period of Hill House corresponds with the
year of *Man and Superman*; both plays credit women as having
greater energy and insight than men, and give this superiority
a cosmic dimension. But what makes the Macdonald sisters
and their imagery significantly different from the 'new woman'
of Shaw's plays and H. G. Wells's novels is the character
of their imagination and its philosophical foundation.

This is seen most easily in their choice of texts for illustration. Maeterlinck's writings are now hard to read with any pleasure: 'he had hit upon a formula for eliciting waves of indefinite yet powerful association by the oblique presentation of people doing simple yet unexplained things in strange and empty places'.[95] Plays such as *La Princesse Maleine* (1889), which inspired Margaret Macdonald's decor for the Warndorfer music salon of 1902, are both melodramatic and static. Yet their subject-matter is sometimes strikingly advanced. *Aglavaine et Sélysette*, for example, which appeared in English in 1897, explores the tensions in a *ménage à trois*, albeit obliquely. In that year an article in *The Studio* specifically linked the work of The Four (and that of Herbert MacNair especially) with 'a return to mysticism, and to superstition and legendary fancies which at first sight seem out of touch with the "actuality" of modernity'.[96] But what appears to be modernity in retrospect is only that aspect of a cultural phase that has managed to survive intact into the present. The subjective idealism of a Maeterlinck or a Macdonald was, in its time, as distinctly modern as the pragmatic energy of the eponymous heroine of H. G. Wells's novel *Ann Veronica* (1909); nor was it unusual for the most new of new men and women to make an apparent reversal. The most spectacular example of this is the sudden conversion in 1889 of Annie Besant, the militant atheist, spokeswoman for birth control and brilliant union organizer, into a Theosophist and the theorist of so-called thought-forms and spiritual drawing.

The Glasgow School of Art was clearly a centrepoint of alternative modernity – its connections with Belgian Symbolism were not solely literary, as I noted earlier. Jean Delville's appointment as professor of painting in 1901 was an ideological signal aligning the School with the resurgence of philosophical and artistic idealism. In *The New Mission of Art* (1900) Delville noted that 'The time has arrived when genius will no longer be unconscious; the genius of the Idealist will, we boldly prophesy, be superconscious'. His concept of an 'Idealist Art' is based on 'the illuminating study of occult psychology', and makes much play with 'vibrations' and 'hierarchies of being'; but it is also infused with a mystical futurism: 'Let the modern artist not forget that a new age is beginning, that the Idea is returning to the earth, and that a purer, fairer, race is about to inhabit the world'. This new age will 'shortly upon the dial of the revolving centuries mark the hour of a universal redemption in the province of thought [in which] Art will break free of nationality'.[97] It is not at all surprising that such ideas were common in 'advanced' and artistic circles; they helped rationalize and relieve grave dilemmas. One writer described Symbolism in its connections with craft and design as offering 'a precarious but immediate solution to the conflict between the life of the spirit and practical life, of which society at the end of the nineteenth century was already acutely aware'.[98]

The 'femininity' of the white interiors should, therefore, be seen as complex and problematical. Their innovative character appears to arise from origins that seem less 'progressive' or emancipatory than they do spiritualist and prophetic.

In Chapter 3, I described Mackintosh's intermediate rooms and hallways, with their fetishized carpentry, as poised between the world as measured and the world as experienced. To descend the stairs of Hill House is to go down from a space that seems larger than it really is through a sort of cage, composed of posts and beams, that becomes progressively more complicated. Entry into the hall below occurs before one is physically in the hall, because the towering posts of the banister and the very large beams of the floor above create a sensed domain that is entered the moment one's line of sight is beneath the floor level of the landing. The cylinder of the stairwell seems to be suddenly intersected by a plane, almost as if one was about to walk into deep water, allowing its surface to close, safely and pleasurably, over one's head.

The distinction between reality as measured and reality as felt is a continuing theme in romanticism, but at the end of the nineteenth century the distinction was an acute philosophical problem, enmeshed with what H. Stuart Hughes has since called a 'sense of the demise of an old society, coupled with an agonizing uncertainty as to what the form of the new society might prove to be'.[99] Hughes describes the attempt by social philosophers to accommodate a sense of the subjective and develop a criticism of earlier methods:

In short, they found themselves inserting between the external data and the final intellectual product an intermediate stage of reflection on their own awareness of these data. The result was an enormous heightening of self-consciousness – a wholesale re-examination of the presuppositions of social thought itself.[100]

Now, there is no simple and direct road from these strictly intellectual matters to the heightened selfconsciousness everywhere displayed by Mackintosh, but the relation between an 'objective' vernacular exterior and the fantastic interior is expressed by those intermediate spaces that 'reflect', anxiously, on the contrasts and tensions inscribed within them, and which call into question our presuppositions about structure. To draw out their full significance we need to follow this road back towards the subject of self-consciousness and the use made of the concept of 'intuition', first in the realm of philosophy and then in more general discourse. Hughes again:

> As a counter balance to the positivist faith in exact science, a number of the young thinkers of the 1890s proposed to rely on 'intuition'. . . . Intuition is not an 'unconscious' process in the Freudian sense; it goes on in the area that Freud called the 'pre-conscious' and William James termed 'the fringe of consciousness'. It is characterized by a 'fusion of intermediate steps' that resists precise indentification. Of its importance 'for all normal symbolic creative thinking, whether artistic of scientific' there can be little doubt. It alone 'makes possible those . . . leaps in art and science by means of which the creative process sometimes dons seven-league boots'.[101]

The relevance of these general intellectual currents to the objects of our study is quite clear. The fusion of intermediate steps or, in Mackintosh's words, the 'integration of myriads of details and circumstances of which (the artworker) cannot be directly conscious', was exactly what Mackintosh demanded of 'the master in every profession'.

In academic philosophy, the movement toward subjectivity was sanctioned and given form by a renewal of Hegelian Idealism. In England this was undertaken by T. H. Green and F. H. Bradley and in Scotland by Bernard Bosanquet, whose *History of Aesthetics* appeared in 1892. This Hegelianism (so much at variance with 'traditional' British thought) was represented in Glasgow by Edward Caird. In his *Hegel* (1883)

Caird was very much concerned with the relations between the spiritual life and materialism, and sought a higher unity that would reconcile these antinomies.[102]

Although there is no direct evidence that Mackintosh read such books, the references to 'synthesis', 'integration' and 'unity' that appear in his lecture notes clearly show that he had an intellectual comprehension of the problems with which he wrestled. And those problems are resolved in these stairwells and halls; the ambivalence of the stairwell in Hill House, of the Library, and even of the Martyr's School, represent an attempt to connect otherwise irreconcilable outer and inner spaces in a unified poetics. And these outers and inners also speak of the dialectic between male and female, between structure and decoration, and between reason and emotion. The synthesis meant, however, the absorption of the subjective into the larger resolution; the artistic sign of this is the disappearance of motifs derived from figurative or pictorial sources, and the gradual development (moving at different paces in different endeavours) of a geometrical style in which constructional motifs progressively replace conventional decoration.

The emblem stencilled in the porch of Hill House may be interpreted in this light: an earlier stage of the dialectic – organic, pictorial (and, it may be, conventionally feminine) – is held in a Euclidean, abstract and 'rational' (male?) frame. The interplay creates the form.

Observed from outside, Hill House is recognizably within the local idiom. What this meant to Mackintosh – and, we must presume, to his client, William Blackie, and his family – is to be learned in an early lecture on 'Scottish Baronial Architecture', which he gave in 1891 at the age of 23; but the persistence of the vernacular in his work – right through until he left Scotland – suggests that the sentiments he expressed in this lecture remained with him. They are sentiments, not arguments: the Baronial style is 'dear to my heart and entwined among my inmost thoughts and affections'; we are drawn to our national architecture through 'instinctive affection'; it is 'as indigenous to our country as our wild flowers, and a product of modern, not classical, history'. The style 'is coming to life again, and I only hope it will not be strangled in its infancy by indiscriminating and unsympathetic people who copy the ancient examples without trying to make [it] conform to modern requirements'.[103]

The idea of an indigenous and pristine architecture that is free of 'styles' and 'copyism', and whose natural 'character' was the 'distinct expression' of the locality was alive throughout Europe in the nineteenth century. The task of every architect that subscribed to it was to remove all the masks that imported cultures had laid on the face of true building, so that the essence of the art could be recovered. Architecture would then be 'natural', and being so would also be good and rational. It would be as universal, and as various, as humanity itself.

The disparity between this ideal and the reality of industrial capitalism was recognized early:

> For as our life is becoming international, a certain uniformity of architectural forms will spread across the globe. We have this uniformity already in our dress. From pole to pole people wear the same jacket and the same blouse. Associations for the conservation of folk dress will not alter this tendency, not will movements to conserve folk art stand in the way of the internationalisation of forms.[104]

The vernacular aspect of Hill House (its exterior) is, therefore, as problematical as its innovative interior. The ironwork of the gate, the stencil in the porch, the finesse of the proportions of the gables, all hint at it: this, they assert, is no ordinary or unselfconscious local idiom. It is as if Mackintosh were saying 'Yes, we are Scots, and we can build a Scots architecture; but only by a deliberate act of will!' The exterior of Hill House is a statement about Nature, but is not itself 'natural'; deliberate selfconsciousness is clearly apparent.

It is this, more than anything, that sets Mackintosh apart from the Arts and Crafts Movement. This Movement was chiefly concerned with realizing concepts of domesticity, craft and architecture that were, supposedly, pre-industrial. It reasserted, both in its moral tone and in its imagery, late eighteenth-century ruralism and the Evangelical belief that, in William Cowper's line in *The Task* (1785), 'God made the country, and man made the town'. The Arts and Crafts Movement sought to return to the roots of the domestic ideology that had helped to form and sustain the lives of the middle classes since the 1820s. It rendered this ideology in brick, stone and good timber with a thoroughness and expense that arose from the enormous economic success of the social groups the ideology had formed and served. It was, in fact, an architecture of self-fulfilment. The best Arts and Crafts houses are among the finest examples of architecture of the nineteenth century, and served as a model for Continental practitioners for many good reasons; but they were devoid of the possibility of real innovation.

In *Das englische Haus* Muthesius explained that the reason for this was a lack of imagination and an insistence on utilitarian and rational principles. Looking at the matter with the benefits of hindsight, this is a charge only partly sustainable. Those architects, Edwin Lutyens especially, now appear to have been highly ingenious and romantic designers; and their utilitarian aspects were at the service of their vision, not at its head. What Muthesius was describing is the undisguised empiricism of their assumptions. Their philosophical roots lie with Locke, and with Rousseau, as transmitted through Ruskin and the tradition of the Picturesque. Thus, the private spaces of an Arts and Crafts house are as commonsensical as the public ones; and the most intimate of their interiors, though frequently pretty and 'feminine' (in the retardaire sense), were carried out with the same practicality and 'honesty' as every other part of the building. Such buildings cannot be seen as offering allegorical journeys. In them there is an admirable integrity; but it closes off access to fantasy and innovation as surely as empiricism and 'common sense' defend the status quo against the demands of the subjective. For the ideologues of the Arts and Crafts Movement, Mackintosh's dialectic and voluntarism were either incomprehensible or threatening. W. H. Bidlake described the 'New Art' as a 'reversion to pre-historic barbarity [that had] detached itself from the past'.[105] His sense of outrage is similar to that which greeted Stravinsky's *Rite of Spring* and Les Fauves. The accusation of barbarism, the confusion between 'reversion' and 'detachment', the undeclared assumptions about 'the past' (what past? whose past?) are the familiar cries of a wounded orthodoxy. It cannot be stressed too strongly that these objections are not simply 'stylistic'; they are ideological. They have to do with conflicting concepts of modernity.

The journey we have made, from within to without, can be repeated in Windyhill, the School of Art and the Mains Street apartment, with the necessary adjustments. Mackintosh did not repeat himself, and there are significant and finely judged differences in tone between the equivalent spaces of these buildings. In each case, the poetics of workmanship is the means by which the affective and ideological dialectic is made manifest.

But before we can make a final assessment of the particular quality of Mackintosh's modernity, we must return to the most intimate interiors and look once again at their problematic aspect.

The feminism of the Glasgow Style operated in a progressive mode. I mean by this that the gender associations are not domestic, and that the stylistic associations are not historical; they may even be, as Muthesius wrote, milestones for a possible future – for the 'purer, fairer' world envisaged by Delville and presented by Geddes as the coming epoch of 'ideal unity'. As they were developed through the poetics of workmanship, these associations imply a relationship between interior and exterior that resolves rather than perpetuates gender antagonism, and sets forth a new ethics of social and private life. This 'progressive mode' is not without its own contradictions and problems, however, which appear to arise from the subjective idealism that underpins it and which is actually at the root of its prophetic force.

The ideology of privacy and the development of modern consumer capitalism are very closely related. This relationship has been little studied as yet because of the conventional distinction between the public and domestic realms that, with its accompanying gender assumptions, has laid greater stress upon production. But any study of design, and especially of interior and domestic design, begins with consumption. As Davidoff and Hall observe:

> the creation of the private sphere has been central to the elaboration of consumer demand, so essential to the expansion and accumulation process which characterizes modern societies.[106]

The domestic sphere (which Davidoff and Hall describe as 'the private') is the main site of consumption, and the nineteenth-century concern with home-making and its virtual invention of the family, as opposed to the household, goes hand in hand with the immense expansion of the manufacture and trade in domestic goods; this, by extension, includes the equally immense development in architectural and allied design. The house, with its fittings and services, furniture, textiles, wallpapers, ornaments and knick-knacks, became a complicated discourse in its own right – the nexus where class, gender, occupation, education and morality were embodied in the array of objects and spaces. It is not too much to say that since the early nineteenth century the main function of design and architecture has been to service this nexus and provide the means to make it possible. Thus, any shift in the relations between public and domestic design, and any extension of that axis of meaning, is certainly related to shifts and extensions in both the means and relations of production and the patterns and rationales of consumption.

The interpretation I am unfolding here is that, as part of a wider 'new art', the work of Mackintosh and Macdonald marks the inward extension of the domestic to include an eroticized and fantastic privacy; and that this was predicated on a subjective idealism incompatible with the philosophical basis of the surrounding domestic ideology, which was principally empiricist and 'common-sense'.[107] We should ask ourselves whether or not the expansion of demand requires the stimulation of subjectivity and the heightening of the sense of self at the expense of 'traditional' social relations. If this is so, we can see that the white interiors make vivid the contradictions lurking within the domestic ideal. The supposedly traditional ideology of domesticity on which the political stability of nation and capital were held to be based, and which was central to the 'expansion and accumulation process', was revealed to contain its opposite – an a-historical and anti-traditional eruption of eroticized selfhood which, while in its progressive mode promises a redefinition of social ethics, in another mode lets loose an insatiable desire for expansive consumption. This second mode proceeds by atomizing the social realm into its smallest parts, destabilizing 'traditional' values and even dissolving established boundaries of gender. It is this second mode that, today, elaborates demand and is predicated upon private consumption rather than on rationalized and socialized production. To put it epigrammatically, fetishization of the commodity is accompanied by fantasization of the self. Seen in this light the subjective idealism that lies at the roots of 'modernism' was far from being emancipatory, for it bound the psychic constitution of each subject still more firmly to the wheel of capital.

Recent years have seen a number of attempts to put together a neo-conservative cultural programme in which domesticity and 'Victorian' values are held to be pre-eminent. This has led to a renewed interest in nineteenth-century design, in all its aspects. This programme 'shifts onto cultural modernism the uncomfortable burdens of a more or less successful capitalist modernization of the economy and society'.[108] But what neo-conservatives deplore as the forces of modernism – 'the principle of unlimited self-realization, the demand for authentic self-experience and the subjectivism of a hyperstimulated sensitivity' – are the very, psychic, dynamics that consumer capitalism requires. This dynamization, linked to utilitarian rationality and colossal technology and sanctioned by a devalued subjective idealism, is the precondition of a successful consumer capitalism.

Empiricism and the domestic ideology provide no basis for this surging energy, and in cleaving to them the Arts and Crafts Movement consigned itself to be the servant of an *ancien régime*. The English rejection of Scots modernity appears, therefore, to be an early instance of the forlorn traditionalism that follows modern capital about like its performing monkey.

Within Britain, this domesticity was itself embedded in an Anglo-centred nationalism that was all the stronger for being largely unspoken; the subjectivity of Mackintosh picked at these assumptions, since it was not just art that, in Delville's phrase, was breaking away from nationality, but the concept of character. Mackintosh's work was not just unhealthy – it was portrayable as foreign, in spite of its Scots nationalism. The long-term consequences of this for him, and for his wife's career too, were severe, since their work not only coincided with increasing chauvinism and the impending Great War, but with the decay of Scottish financial autonomy, which in turn eroded the possibilities of an autonomous architectural expression. The lamentable end of the 'distinct expression' of Scots identity – a demise that has recently been described very exactly –[109] came in the Scottish Exhibition of National History, Art and Industry held in Glasgow in 1911, complete with 'Highland Village' and an 'Auld Toon'; the Mackintoshes' contribution to this event was limited to the interior of the tea-room.

There is a further element in Mackintosh that made the

demise of the project more likely; an element that was part of the aesthetic debate. In general terms, forms of subjective idealism were part of that generation of what has subsequently come to be called 'Modernism'. These forms either acted as a catalyst in the creation of new styles or remained an essential feature of the work of particular artists and architects. But in every case this idealism was linked with a non-Associationist or 'absolutist' aesthetics, in which there are 'constants of expression', universally valid symbolisms of colour and shape that constitute the 'foundation' of all art, and a consequent attachment to 'primary' forms and colours.[110] This was a position Mackintosh rejected as among the 'props' of art.

Investigation shows that these ideas represent a reworking of much older ideas in the light of a similar movement in the early part of the nineteenth century; an idealism in scientific dress that should be thought of as a transformation of the academic into the industrial. This form of idealism returned aesthetic speculation and artistic practice right back toward scientism and the fetishization of the machine. In no-one is this more marked than in Le Corbusier, whose early intellectual and artistic experience has close parallels to that of Mackintosh.[111] In strictly theoretical terms, the Associationist aesthetics with which Mackintosh was early imbued made this step more difficult.

The increasing abstraction of the later decoration – the first manifestations of which were at Hill House and in the Scotland Street School – appear to be steps in this direction. In the case of the Hill House table (illus. 51), the origin of the motifs is no longer pictorial; it is, as we have seen, auto-reflective, embodying an overall constructive principle in miniature. In the case of the Scotland Street School, the origins of the square and triangle motifs lie in the gigantic emblem on the south façade, which turns a Scottish thistle into the Tree of Life (illus. 72); the treatment of the thistle cone provides for combinations of squares and triangles that, continued round to the front of the School, lose their local associations and become wholly abstract (illus. 73). Mackintosh's earlier decoration was associational, with its origins in art botany and the human body; but the later development of his style into geometric abstraction had no such clear poetics.

The problem for Mackintosh, and for any study of his later

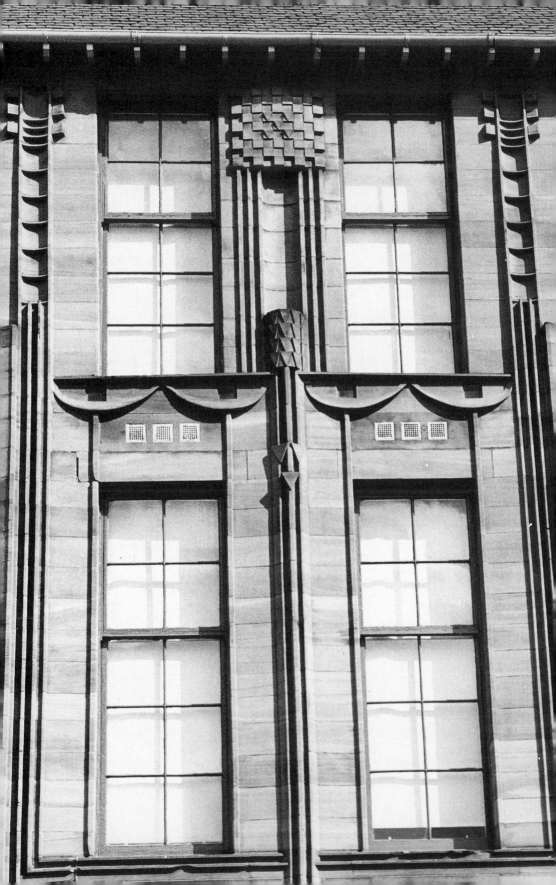

72 Mackintosh's Thistle-cum-Tree of Life motif on the south (rear) façade of his Scotland Street School, Glasgow (1904-6).

73 Decorative detail designed by Mackintosh for the north (main) façade of Scotland Street School.

work, is one of association. As a young man, in 1893, and taking his phrases from Lethaby and César Daly, he asked for 'a symbolism immediately comprehensible by the great majority of spectators'.[112] Nine years later, in 'Seemliness', he made a distinction between symbolism and 'the creative imagination'. Symbolism, at least of the direct and emblematic kind to be found in applied motifs, is seen to be inferior to the 'power of invention'. The distinction Mackintosh was making is similar to that which was made many years before by Christopher Dresser. Ornament, Dresser argued, embodies 'Mind'; the use of a symbolism based upon common belief is no longer valid. 'We cannot hope that symbolism will again prevail . . . [we need to develop a decorative style] to express thoughts, feelings and ideas without the aid of recognised symbols . . . such as induce the mind to create to itself given thoughts . . . to manifest the possibility of ideas being expressed by conventional forms without the aid of symbols.'[113] Dresser then finds himself involved in musical analogies and quasi-scientific arguments about form and sound and vibration, and early instance of ideas later taken up by painters such as Kandinsky.

Mackintosh, in his 'Seemliness' notes, is wrestling with this problem, which he identifies as 'the task of clothing in grace

133

and beauty the new forms and conditions that modern developments of life – social – commercial and religious insist upon – '. But he lacked the conceptual models that were available to Continental practitioners. The Associationist aesthetic, his nationalism, his loyalty to Arts and Crafts ideas and phraseology – all stood in the way of his formulating a clear statement of the problems attendant upon moving from an emblematic decoration and an 'immediately comprehensible' architectural symbolism towards the greater abstraction and synthesis that his fundamental practice demanded. There is an accent of desperate exasperation in the finale of these notes: ' – flowers that grow from but above the green leaf – flowers that are not dead – are not dying – not artificial – real flowers springing from your own soul – '. Here Mackintosh appears to be arguing for an end to Aestheticism and subjective idealism; but he is not able to say in what the meaning of a new grace and beauty will consist.

In fact, idealism and the neo-occult served as an effective, though temporary, validation for Continental artists and architects, because the models of universality they offered could serve as steps toward a style for the coming century that, for good or ill, was undecorated, abstract, cosmopolitan, non-associational and (at least in principle) based upon universally available technology. The decline of Mackintosh's career, the eclipse of the Glasgow Style, the retirement of Margaret Macdonald from practice – all had many causes, personal, professional and economic; but among them is a dilemma of a fundamental kind that was not peculiar to Mackintosh.

The idea of a 'modernism' has normally been taken to imply an 'internationalism' that excludes regional or national references. The term 'International Style' was proudly adopted during the 1930s for polemical reasons; it marked a sharp differentiation between the progressive and the nationalist tendencies. It was adopted or put upon architects and designers of different character, working in very different circumstances. If we identify 'modernism' with the International Style and its subsequent commercial extrapolation, and then reify it as the Modern Movement, we are mistaking polemic for reality. A similar confusion has arisen in painting, in which the term 'modernism' has come to be identified with a particular theory of the course of painting put forward by critics such as Clement Greenberg. But it is important to clear the mind of propaganda and to look at the substance; and when we do that, we see that there are always several 'modernisms' colliding, interlocking or running on parallel tracks, and that particular designs can partake of one or more of these alternatives. By modernism, I mean a well-considered and positive attempt to embrace contemporary conditions of production, use and theory. What comprises 'modern conditions' will depend on where we are, and when, since the concept assumes continual changes. Thus 'modernism', as an inclusive concept, cannot be identified with any style or particular period, and can only be plural in its expressions. Mackintosh's modernism is of an especially interesting and instructive kind. It comprises the most advanced with the most local. It attempts to resolve gender antagonisms of the most stubborn kind, and it exemplifies the general concerns and dilemmas of industrial world culture in the specific and particular mode of the city and the region.

For our own day, Kenneth Frampton has imagined a 'critical regionalism' in which an architecture could be developed that respected the site and the region, that was craftsmanlike and sensuously satisfying, but which would in no sense be retardaire or anachronistic:

> Architecture can only be sustained today as a critical practice if it assumes as 'arriere-garde' position, that is to say, one which distances itself equally from the Enlightenment myth of progress and from a reactionary, unrealistic impulse to return to the architectonic forms of the preindustrial past . . . [it] has to remove itself from both the optimization of advanced technology and the ever present tendency to regress into nostalgic historicism or the glibly decorative.

A critical regionalism is seen as poised between a world culture and the universal civilization of industry:

> it has to 'deconstruct' the overall spectrum of world culture which it inevitably inherits [and] it has to achieve, through synthetic contradiction, a manifest critique of universal civilization.[114]

It would be a risky exercise to project today's concerns back upon the Glasgow of 1900, yet the idea of a 'critical' regionalism sits well on Mackintosh as compared to his English contemporaries. The nationalistic domesticity of the Arts and Crafts Movement could not develop because it was entirely absorbed within its own ideology. But the designs I have discussed were continuously, and knowingly, poised between contraries. It was the critical tension within the work that made Mackintosh significant throughout Europe and, finally, unacceptable at home.

AFTERWORD

The direction of this essay has been toward our most pressing cultural problem: how to resolve the antinomies of the local and the global. How is a modern humanity to be realized? According to Paul Ricoeur:

> The phenomenon of universalization, while being an advancement of mankind, at the same time constitutes a sort of subtle destruction, not only of traditional cultures, which might not be an irreparable wrong, but also of what I shall call for the time being the creative nucleus of great cultures, that nucleus on the basis of which we interpret life, what I shall call in advance the ethical and mythical nucleus of mankind.[115]

The fear – 'that we should lose all expression' – inspired the movements of national and regional revivalism and the antiquarian passion for local craft-building. This brought about a flowering of domestic and related architecture and design whose consequences ran all through the industrial world. In a broad sense, this reaction to the universalizing power of industry, technology and capital is typical; it is repeated in its essential form wherever a powerful existing culture comes up against global transformation. The shock of this induces an equally powerful reaction toward some version of the 'ethical and mythical nucleus'.

I write 'some version', because these reactions are never ideologically neutral. The 'nucleus' of a culture is not given in some unproblematic history; it is defined through incessant struggling, in which scholarship has a role to play. Moreover, these reactions are always under the threat of hysteria and the passion for authority. We should see these negative symptoms not as an aberration of modern societies but as a constant and permanent possibility that can take both violent and legal forms, and which can creep in through democratic legislation just as surely as through fascism and the threat of war.

The realization of the ethical and mythical dimensions of life is a necessity, but they are not simply there to be picked out of 'traditional' practice, out of 'myth', as if out of a lucky-dip. There is nothing more illustrative of that subtle destruction than the easy assumption that there are real and substantial traditions, viable myths and a usable history; such thinking is, truly understood, an instance of the commodification of culture it purports to oppose. In modern conditions of production and consumption, a true realization of the nucleus of life can only be achieved through a critical understanding of the tensions inherent in continuous world-transformation. If we do not feel we are being torn apart, then we are not experiencing reality. And this, in sum, is why the work we have been looking at is important, because, within the terms of its time, it met these tensions and resolved them in the creation of beautiful buildings and interiors. Their special character and content was a product of a critical clash between the specific ideas and practices of the time and of the place, and those irresponsible powers of transformation. The purpose of that artistic project, in which a critical consciousness was a primary and necessary condition, was the realization of a modern life.

References

1. H. Muthesius, *Das englische Haus*, 3 vols (Berlin, 1904–5), trans. J. Seligman (London, 1979), p. 52.

2. F. Ahlers-Hestermann, quoted in N. Pevsner, *Studies in Art, Architecture and Design* (London, 1968), II, p. 161.

3. Shand, in a letter to William Davidson, 31st March 1933; quoted in J. Burkhauser, *The Glasgow Girls: Women in Art and Design, 1880–1920*, exhibition catalogue (Glasgow, 1990), p. 115.

4. R. Macleod, *Charles Rennie Mackintosh: Architect and Artist* (Glasgow, 1968, revd 1983), p. 7.

5. Macleod, *Mackintosh*, p. 149.

6. I am here indebted to D. Daiches, *Glasgow* (London, 1977), Ch. 12. This unusual development was made viable by the development of an extensive and advanced system of tramways and omnibus routes, at first horsedrawn and later (from 1898) electric: 'in their heyday [they] were the equal of any in the world and had a good claim to be the world's best'. This, in turn, was supported by a subway, effective from 1897.

7. See F. Alison, *Charles Rennie Mackintosh as a Designer of Chairs* (London, 1978), p. 5.

8. The only record I have been able to trace consists of four old photographs now in the National Maritime Museum, London, of which illus. 2 is one.

9. Documentation of the *Livadia* has been collected and published in pamphlet form, edited by Lewis Welford (London, 1977).

10. The contract books of Fairfield's Yard are in the U.S.C. archive of the Mitchell Library, Glasgow. The Caird archives have vanished. Research into this area is difficult, since designs are designated by job numbers rather than by the names of contractors, while the designers and architects are never mentiond. For the *Fürst Bismarck* (Yard no. 438), we also find payments to John Crawford for carving, to J. D. Heymann for cabinet work, to Galbraith and Winton for tile-work, etc. It is clear that this is an interesting field for the design historian, and I regret that I have not had the opportunity to investigate it more fully.

11. M. Donnelly, *Glasgow Stained Glass: A Preliminary Study* (Glasgow, 1981), p. 17. I am also indebted to conversations with this author.

12. See P. Robertson, ed., *Charles Rennie Mackintosh: The Architectural Papers* (Glasgow, 1990), p. 208.

13. For a useful discussion of this topic see R. Banham, *The Architecture of the Well-tempered Environment* (London, 1969), pp. 84-6.

14. P. Geddes, *Cities in Evolution* (1915), quoted in P. Boardman, *The Worlds of Patrick Geddes* (London, 1978), p. 200.

15. For a discussion of Taylor's career, see G. Larner and C. Larner, *The Glasgow Style* (Glasgow, 1980), pp. 16–8.

16. 'Design' in this context being the decorative arts. These figures are taken from the *British Association . . . Handbook for Glasgow*, edited by M. Maclean and published at Glasgow on the occasion of the 1901 Exhibition.

17. The case of James Lavery is instructive: one of the most 'French' of the Irish and Scots painters of the period, he studied in Paris and was

influenced by Bastien-Lepage and the *plein-air* School. His best work was produced during his Glasgow years, but his facility as a society portrait painter proved to be his artistic undoing. For a more complete account, see R. Billcliffe, *The Glasgow Boys*, exhibition catalogue (Glasgow, 1985). The inability of the Glasgow Boys to get further than they did is also worth some study; the decline of this group around 1910 matches the occlusion of the Glasgow Style. (See also the Scottish Arts Council's exhibition catalogue, *The Glasgow Boys*, 2 parts, Glasgow, 1968.)

18. Quoted in Larner and Larner, *The Glasgow Style*, p. 2.

19. For painting, the development of the 'carpet paradigm' was related to the earlier debate about the organization of patterns for carpets and wall-hangings. Flat non-representational patterns (Owen Jones) or shallow emblematic designs (Pugin) were an essential part of 'advanced' taste. One of the most vehement assertions of this doctrine was also the earliest: 'The soul of the apartment is the carpet. From it are deduced not only the hues but the forms of all objects incumbent. . . . Touching pattern . . . distinct grounds, and vivid and cycloid features, of no meaning, are here Median laws. The abomination of flowers, or representation of well-known objects of any kind, should not be endured . . .' (E. A. Poe, *The Philosophy of Furniture*, 1840). See J. Maschek, 'The Carpet Paradigm: Prolegomena to a Theory of Flatness', *Arts Magazine* [New York] (September 1976).

20. Recent published research has made the origins of the Glasgow Style much clearer; see Burkhauser, *The Glasgow Girls*.

21. A useful source-book is W. Hipple, *The Beautiful, the Sublime and the Picturesque in Eighteenth-century British Aesthetic Theory* (Carbondale, Illinois, 1957). See also George Hershey, *High Victorian Gothic: A Study in Associationism* (London, 1972).

22. See, especially, E. R. de Zurko, *Origins of Functionalist Theory* (New York, 1957).

23. See Hershey, *High Victorian Gothic*, for an extended discussion, especially of the Ecclesiological Movement.

24. See Robertson, ed., *The Architectural Papers*, p. 223.

25. See R. McFadzean, *The Life and Work of Alexander Thomson* (London, 1979), p. 103.

26. Ibid., p. 102.

27. Ibid., p. 107.

28. A. Gomme and D. Walker, *The Architecture of Glasgow* (London, 1968), p. 204.

29. Ibid., p. 114.

30. Between 1884 and 1907 Templeton bought over twenty paintings for sums equivalent to many thousands of pounds at today's prices, and his personal ledgers record a collection of satsuma ware, Japanese and Persian *objets d'art*, and fine furniture. He invested in steamships, gold-mining, silk-weaving and American railroads – and, of course, in his own carpet business. Templeton's ledgers are in the Business Records section of the University of Glasgow Archives.

31. Paul Ricoeur, 'Universal Civilization and National Cultures', in *History and Truth*, trans. C. A. Kibley (Evanston, 1965), p. 277.

32. R. Wornum, 'The Exhibition as a Lesson in Taste', in *The Illustrated Catalogue of the Great Exhibition* (1851). This essay is discussed in Pevsner, *Studies*.

33. See Macleod, *Mackintosh*, Ch. 1, for a useful discussion, and D. M. Walker, 'Mackintosh's Scottish Antecedents', in P. Nuttgens, ed., *Mackintosh and his Contemporaries in Europe and America* (London, 1988).

34. From Mackintosh's lecture on 'Scottish Baronial Architecture' (1891); see Robertson, ed., *The Architectural Papers*, pp. 51–2.

35. See K. Frampton, 'Toward a Critical Regionalism: Six Points for an Architecture of Resistance', in H. Foster, ed., *Postmodern Culture* (London, 1985), pp. 16–30.

36. Owen Jones, *The Grammar of Ornament* (London, 1856), p. 154.

37. For discussion of this Associationism, see Hershey, *High Victorian Gothic*, Ch. 1.

38. For a discussion of this and the letters of Warrington Taylor, see M. Girouard, *Sweetness and Light: The Queen Anne Movement, 1860–1900* (Oxford, 1977), pp. 18ff.

39. For a mischievous dissection of these moralisms, see B. C. Brolin, *Flight of Fancy: The Banishment and Return of Ornament* (London, 1985).

40. Jones, *The Grammar of Ornament*, p. 154. Jones actually confuses his first proposition – 'The Decorative Arts arise from . . . Architecture' – by arguing in the final chapter that 'architecture adopts ornament, does not create it.'

41. Ibid., p. 156.

42. For a more detailed discussion, see D. Brett, 'The Interpretation of Ornament', *Journal of Design History*, I/2 (1988), pp. 103–12.

43. The Chairman's Address (1885), quoted in W. Buchanan, ed., *Mackintosh's Masterwork: The Glasgow School of Art* (Glasgow, 1989), p. 15.

44. Forbes, in *'The Art Journal' Illustrated Catalogue of the Great Exhibition* (London, 1851).

45. J. Ruskin, *The Eagle's Nest* (1872), paras 148–50, 171–2ff.

46. See Brett, 'The Interpretation of Ornament' (1988).

47. W. Eadie, in his *Movements of Modernity: The Case of Glasgow and Art Nouveau* (London, 1990), devotes several valuable pages to this topic, especially pp. 154-70.

48. Schleiden was Professor of Botany at the University of Jena, and one of the founders of modern scientific botany. He was responsible for awarding Christopher Dresser his doctorate. His popular book, *The Plant: A Biography*, appeared in English in 1848. See Brett, 'The Interpretation of Ornament' (1988). The subject of nineteenth-century popular botany has been explored by Nicolette Scourse, *The Victorians and their Flowers* (London, 1983).

49. See Robertson, ed., *The Architectural Papers*, p. 224.

50. The 'Roaring Camp' and related matters have been examined most recently in Burkhauser, ed., *The Glasgow Girls*, by several contributors.

51. For relevant material see M. Tuchman, ed., *The Spiritual in Art: Abstract Painting, 1890–1985*, exhibition catalogue, Los Angeles County Museum of Art (1987), in which plates from the works of Jacob Boehme are reproduced. As I have indicated in the opening chapter, there were many connections between the Glasgow avant-garde and painters in The Netherlands and Belgium. In this, as in so many cases, we see neo-occultism acting as midwife at the birth of the 'new art'.

52. The Association has no membership records of that period; they kindly allowed me to look over their uncatalogued library, which is full of relevant literature but has nothing that seems to me to be directly connected with graphic representation.

53. See Boardman, *The Worlds of Patrick Geddes*, p. 143. Geddes was particularly interested in graphic expressions of natural and social processes; in this case he was employing neo-occult imagery. Around this time he was reading Edouard Schuré's *The Great Initiates* (see Boardman, p. 194).

54. There is clearly a playful element at work. See, for example, the description of the *Cabbages* watercolour printed in the School of Art's magazine and in R. Billcliffe, *Mackintosh Watercolours* (London, 1978), p. 28. But jests can be serious as well. In a similar way, the fairy themes

of the Macdonald sisters take up an earlier nineteenth-century genre; which used Fairyland as a metaphor for sexual shenanigans.

55. As paraphrased by D. Howarth, *Charles Rennie Mackintosh and the Modern Movement* (London, 1952, revd 1977), pp. 19–22.

56. See R. Billcliffe, *Architectural Sketches and Flower Drawings by Charles Rennie Mackintosh* (London, 1977), for illustrations of these and other works.

57. This excess could take on a character that manages to be both ecstatic and kitsch at the same time, as when George Logan, one of the minor figures of the Glasgow Style, designed a bower full of roses and wrote of the symphonic values of 'colour music' with reference, first, to the Temple of David and Solomon and, second, to some sketches of a boudoir for Messrs Wylie & Lochead. See *The Studio* (November, 1905), pp. 118–22, for an article and drawings entitled *A Colour Symphony* by George Logan. The Larners, in *The Glasgow Style*, suspect that 'George Logan' may have been a fiction.

58. In Semper's inaugural address to the Dresden Academy in 1836 he referred to 'palaeo-zoology': 'A method analogous to that which Cuvier followed, applied to art and especially to architecture, would at last contribute toward getting a clear insight over its whole province, and perhaps also form the base of a doctrine of style, and a sort of topic, or method – How to Invent'. See P. Collins, 'The Biological Analogy', *Architectural Review*, CXXVI (1959), L. Ettlinger, 'On Science, Industry and Art', *Architectural Review*, CXXXVI (1964), and P. Steadman, *The Evolution of Designs* (Cambridge, 1979).

59. For a discussion of biological analogy in design ideas, see my unpublished doctoral thesis (Royal College of Art, London, 1984).

60. For Idealist and Symbolist elements in botanical science, see P. C. Ritterbush, *Overtures to Biology* (New Haven, 1964), and A. Arber, *The Natural Philosophy of Plant Form* (Cambridge, 1950). Christopher Dresser's own botanical writings are very definitely part of the intermediary zone between science and mysticism. For him, 'Vegetable nature may be viewed in another light . . . and this is a poetic and artistic or ornamental light'. The full title of the book published in 1860 from which this quotation comes, is *Unity in Variety: As deduced from the vegetable kingdom, being an attempt at developing that oneness which is discoverable in the habits, modes of growth and principles of construction of all plants.* Schematic illustrations from this book are reproduced in his *Principles of Decorative Design* (1873). See Brett, 'The Interpretation of Ornament' (1988).

61. L. Sullivan, *A System of Architectural Ornament* (reprinted New York, 1967).

62. J. Habermas, *Knowledge and Human Interests*, trans. J. J. Schapiro (London, 2nd edn, 1978), pp. 71 and 80. See Brett, 'The Interpretation of Ornament' (1988).

63. F. Ahlers-Hestermann, quoted in N. Pevsner, 'Charles Rennie Mackintosh', *Studies*, II. The full quotation is fascinating, and its use in Pevsner's wonderful essay on Mackintosh is very apt.

64. Pevsner, 'Charles Rennie Mackintosh', in *Studies*, II, p. 162.

65. 'Seemliness' (1902); see Robertson, ed., *The Architectural Papers*, p. 221.

66. G. Bachelard, *The Poetics of Space* (Boston, 1969), first published in Paris in 1958, and other writings. Especially relevant is Bachelard's concept of 'topoanalysis – the systematic psychological study of the sites of our intimate lives' (ibid., p. 8).

67. Illustrated in Buchanan, ed., *Mackintosh's Masterwork*, p. 84.

68. *C. R. Mackintosh: The Complete Furniture* (Guildford, 1979), p. 209.

69. The most succinct account of the immediate sources of these lectures is in David Walker's contribution, 'Mackintosh on Architecture', to

Robertson, ed., *The Architectural Papers*. Walker shows how completely Mackintosh was ignoring the Beaux-Arts ambiance of his contemporaries and independently chose Ruskin, Morris, Sedding and Lethaby for his guides. Lectures such as the untitled paper of 1892 and 'Architecture' of 1893 follow directly upon Morris's reprinting of Ruskin's *The Nature of Gothic* in 1891, the publication of Lethaby's *Architecture, Mysticism and Myth* (1891), recent lectures by Sedding and Morris and the publication of *Arts and Crafts Essays* by Sedding (1893). Walker makes it clear how extremely well-read Mackintosh was in the relevant literature, how ruthlessly he used it, and how he deliberately ignored everything else.

70. A clear account of Lethaby's influence has been given by Robert Macleod, 'Lethaby as a Key to Mackintosh', in Nuttgens, ed., *Mackintosh and his Contemporaries*, pp. 18–24.

71. Some of the earlier photographs of the School of Art show exposed – unshaded – light bulbs, which suggests that the original shades were perhaps not very effective with the low illumination then available.

72. Buchanan, ed., *Mackintosh's Masterwork*, p. 33.

73. In what follows I am developing ideas set out in D. Brett, 'The Eroticisation of Domestic Space: A Mirror by C. R. Mackintosh', *The Journal of Decorative and Propaganda Arts* (Fall, 1988), pp. 6–13.

74. Ibid.

75. The use of secondary and tertiary colours by the Aesthetic Movement was a deliberate reference to the South Kensington doctrine – that civilizations used primary colours in their energetic youth and declined into mixed hues later. The 'greenery-yallery' and lilac attributes of 'decadence' were being deliberately and provocatively used by the Glasgow Style to assert a new art for a new life.

76. The degree to which Macdonald is a presence as an 'immured figure' in the erotic iconography of the rooms is also a matter for surmise. The female figures in Mackintosh's paintings and decorative designs do often resemble her, and the ample and rather grand proportions of some features and motifs suggest a tall and stately woman, such as she is known to have been. See the discussion by Timothy Neat in Burkhauser, ed., *The Glasgow Girls*, pp. 152ff.

77. Billcliffe, *Mackintosh: The Complete Furniture*, p. 80.

78. The most extreme of the white interiors now surviving are certainly the Mackintoshes' own. The master bedrooms in Hill House and Windyhill, though richer in colour, are more restrained in form and imagery, while the Hill House living-room is more robust.

79. I am not, of course, attempting any detailed or orthodox analysis here. It may be that in Kleinian terms this lack of differentiation and benevolent fantasy, to which I attribute the genesis of the white interiors, is the realm of the 'good objects' that ward off anxiety. This passage is, in general, indebted to the writings of Adrian Stokes and Anton Ehrenzweig. It might also be developed in relation to Julia Kristeva's concept of the 'semiotic' and pre-Oedipal experience. It is interesting that Ruskin identifies an undifferentiated vision with the 'infantine' method of seeing, which every artist must struggle to regain (see *The Elements of Drawing*, 1859, especially the Introduction).

80. P. Geddes and J. Arthur Thompson, *The Evolution of Sex* (London, 1889), especially Ch. 19 and p. 281. What these two proposed is something very like a dialectical materialism, and their argument can be related to the more recent writings of Sebastiano Timpanaro.

81. See Boardman, *The Worlds of Patrick Geddes*, p. 117.

82. See Burkhauser, ed., *The Glasgow Girls*, p. 68.

83. 'Seemliness' (1902); see Robertson, ed., *The Architectural Papers*, p. 223.

84. Mackintosh, paraphrasing Lethaby; see Robertson, ed., *The Architectural Papers*, p. 206.

85. Muthesius, *Das englische Haus*, p. 52. The complaint that the white furniture was also flimsily made (recently repeated by Gavin Stamp) does seem to be well founded. Those pieces that have not been cared for are frequently in poor condition, but the charge of poor workmanship cannot be laid to the *oeuvre* as a whole: after a century of hard use and few repairs, the School of Art demonstrates the robustness of its workmanship. As for the 'impracticality' of the white interiors, every age has its own notion of the practical (to what degree is a Rococo boudoir 'practical'?), just as it has its own notion of comfort. The modern woman, looking at the Mains Street living-room, says 'How the devil did she keep it clean?' There are three points to be made about this. First, we know that Mackintosh worked very closely with his clients (he actually went to live with the Davidson family during the design of Windyhill, and consulted with them in detail about each room); we must assume the clients thought his designs were 'practical'. Second, we should also regard the white rooms as exploiting the new cleanliness offered by electric light; one of the functions of elaborate mouldings and applied decoration was to disguise the grime of oil and gas lamps. To us they may appear impractical, but at the time they must have seemed the expression of a new freedom from soot. Third, his clients had professional servants and cleaners. The style of the rooms implies, of course, a refined manner of life; but is there any extreme style that does not? Mackintosh and Macdonald, in the days of their first success, dressed to complement their rooms: she in the Aesthetic manner and he in a style that was both clerical and dandified. There are several accounts of their appearance and personal style, in which there is a definite hint of humour; photographs suggest that Margaret was a rather grand young woman, but they make Mackintosh look both dreamy and waspish. (None of the photographs, of course, can reveal his pronounced limp, which one interviewee referred to as a 'club foot'.)

86. In a recent study of Beardsley it is argued that his imagery is a sustained and deliberate promotion of the New Woman rather than *fin de siècle* perversity. Linda Zatlin's *Aubrey Beardsley and Victorian Sexual Politics* (Oxford, 1990) contains much material that is relevant for a better understanding of the Glasgow Style. The same charges in the same language were laid against both, for similar reasons. The significant difference is, however, that the imagery of new womanhood in Glasgow was being created by the women themselves.

87. D. L. Silverman, *Art Nouveau in 'Fin de Siècle' France: Politics, Psychology and Style* (Berkeley, 1989). This work and the doctoral thesis on which it is based (Princeton University, 1983) are necessary reading for an overall understanding of these questions, but provide only an imperfect guide to the development of Art Nouveau outside France. My quotation is from Silverman's thesis (1983), p. 121. See also Brett, 'The Interpretation of Ornament' (1988), and Brett, 'The Eroticisation of Domestic Space' (1988).

88. That the Secession was partly financed by the Wittgenstein family seem to bear this out. See the studies by C. E. Schorske, *Fin de Siècle Vienna: Politics and Culture* (New York, 1981), and A. Janik and S. Toulmin, *Wittgenstein's Vienna* (New York, 1973). In Belgium, Art Nouveau was associated with left-wing politics; in Barcelona, the 'modernism' of Domènech and Gaudí had nationalist overtones.

89. Silverman (1983), p. 149.

90. Note that 'believers hoped that a scientific epistemology would verify the materiality of the unseen world whilst at the same time exposing the

paucity of a militant scientism which espoused a barren materialist philosophy. Spiritualists opposed what they regarded as the gross materialism of an age in which things of the spirit no longer had relevance, but proposed a new metaphysical cosmology based upon a (albeit rarified) form of matter. Similarly, whilst the spiritualist project signalled the inadequacy of the empiricist/scientific method, it was itself entirely enmeshed in its terms' (Alex Owen, *The Darkened Room: Women, Power and Spiritualism in Late Nineteenth-century England* (London, 1989), Introduction, also pp. 4 and 10). There are some truly devastating comments on this attempt to have your cake and eat it in Lenin's *Materialism and Empirio-criticism* (1909).

91. T. Gibbons, 'British Abstract Painting of the 1860s', *Modern Painters*, (Summer 1988), pp. 33–7. Automatic writing was also part of W. B. Yeats's inspiration, while automatic drawing and writing both feature in Surrealism.

92. The Glasgow Association of Spiritualists (founded 1867) has, unfortunately, no detailed records. For Mondrian's paintings of women and their Theosophical references see, most recently, Herbert Henkels, 'Mondrian in his Studio', in *Mondrian: From Figuration to Abstraction*, exhibition catalogue, The Tokyo Shimbun (1987).

93. Here I am indebted to T. R. Wright, whose *The Religion of Humanity: The Impact of Comtean Positivism on Victorian Britain* (Cambridge, 1986) has provided me with relevant material.

94. This internalized female should, preferably, be a real woman; but an historical, or even an imaginary, figure will suffice as an object for concentration: 'All this comprises the Positivist model of private worship, whilst its public worship focuses upon woman as a symbolic figure, representative of Humanity herself'. Ibid., pp. 35–6.

95. Roger Cardinal, in J. Wintle, ed., *Makers of Nineteenth-century Culture, 1800–1914* (London, 1982).

96. Gleeson White, in *The Studio*, IV (1897), p. 256.

97. Jean Delville, *The New Mission of Art: A Study of Idealism in Art*, trans. F. Colmar with introductory notes by Clifford Bax and Edward Schuré (London, 1910), pp. xx, xxviii, 10, 61, 74, 182. The first edition was published in Brussels in 1900 and was presumably known to the governors of the School of Art at the time they appointed Delville. According to M. L. Frongia, 'These theories were deepened during the years of his long stays in "Inghilterra" from 1900 to 1907' (*Il simbolismo di Jean Delville*, Bologna, 1978). The same title was given to an address that Delville gave to an assembly of the Theosophical Society in Amsterdam in 1905. Edouard Schuré, a key link in neo-occultism, was the author of *The Great Initiates*, whose readers included Patrick Geddes, Mondrian and Le Corbusier. The publishing history of *The Great Initiates* is extensive: following publication in Paris in 1889 it appears to have had 220 editions in many languages. A recent edition is that by Harper & Row (San Francisco, 1961) for Rudolf Steiner Publications.

98. Oreste Ferrari, in *The McGraw Encyclopaedia of World Art* (New York, 1959), under 'Symbolism'.

99. H. Stuart Hughes, *Consciousness and Society: The Reorientation of European Social Thought, 1890–1930* (London, 1979), p. 14.

100. Ibid., p. 26.

101. Ibid., p. 30. Hughes is quoting L. S. Kubie in *Psychoanalysis as Science*, ed. E. Pumpian-Mindlin (Stanford, 1952), pp. 50–1. The writings of Bosanquet, Caird and others have already been noted. Another relevant text is William James, *The Varieties of Religious Experience* (1902).

102. Eadie, in *Movements of Modernity*, has made the fascinating discovery that Francis Newbery was attempting to link the School of Art with the

University of Glasgow, of which Caird's brother, John, was Principal (pp. 172ff). Eadie sees the School as enabling the traditional dualism that had separated the intellect from the passions to be bypassed and the Glasgow Art Nouveau movement to appear. But I think he credits Mackintosh with greater intellectual self-awareness and consistency than our knowledge of him warrants.

103. See Robertson, ed., *The Architectural Papers*, p. 63.

104. In the context of the debate about standardization that occupied the Deutscher Werkbund, see J. Posener, 'Hermann Muthesius', *The Architects' Yearbook* (1962).

105. W. H. Bidlake, 'The Home from Outside', in *The Modern Home*, ed. W. S. Sparrow (?1906), p. 22. The Glasgow Style was also strongly associated, in English minds, with the world of *The Yellow Book* and the trial of Oscar Wilde. English artistic circles spent a great deal of energy avoiding the imputation of indecency!

106. See L. Davidoff and C. Hall, *Family Fortunes: Men and Women of the English Middle Class, 1780–1850* (London, 1987), especially Ch. 3.

107. See D. Brett, 'Drawing and the Ideology of Industrialization', *Design Issues*, III (Fall 1986), pp. 59–72.

108. J. Habermas, 'Modernity – An Incomplete Project', in *Postmodern Culture*, ed. H. Foster (London, 1985).

109. I am here indebted to Eadie, *Movements in Modernity*, pp. 232–3.

110. Here one thinks of De Stijl, of Purism and of Kandinsky's theories among many examples; the literature is very extensive.

111. The Jura School, regionalism, craft practice, the teaching of L'Eplattenier, *The Grammar of Ornament*, neo-occultism, Edouard Schuré, etc.

112. Robertson, ed., *The Architectural Papers*, p. 206.

113. Christopher Dresser, 'The Art of Decorative Design', *The Builder*, XV (March 1862), pp. 185–6. See also Dresser's book of the same title published in the same year, in which these ideas are amplified.

114. K. Frampton, 'Towards a Critical Regionalism: Six Points for an Architecture of Resistance', in *Postmodern Culture*, ed. H. Foster (London, 1985), pp. 16–30.

115. In *History and Truth*, as quoted by Frampton, op. cit.

The Mackintosh literature is now very large; extensive bibliographies can be found in Buchanan, ed., *Mackintosh's Masterwork*; J. Cooper, ed., *Mackintosh Architecture: The Complete Buildings and Selected Projects* (London, 1978); Eadie, *Movements of Modernity*; and the 1990 paperback reprint of the revised edition (1977) of Howarth, *Charles Rennie Mackintosh*.

Since 1973 the Charles Rennie Mackintosh Society has published a regular Newsletter, which includes details of all kinds of coverage and developments that relate to the architect's life and works. The growth of interest in Mackintosh over the past few years is such that the architect's incompleted designs for 'A House for a Lover of Art' – submitted in 1901 to a competition launched by the German magazine *Zeitschrift für Innendekoration* – have finally been taken up by a consortium of sponsors: in 1989 construction of the Art Lover's House began in Bellahouston Park, Glasgow.

Chronology

Some details of Mackintosh's life would repay further investigation: for
example, the drawing tours that Mackintosh seems to have undertaken
nearly every year of his working life, and the architectural and botanical
motifs he gathered in the course of them. These were an important part
of the rhythm of his life and work. It is sensible to base a chronology
around the design of the buildings, but the reader should remember that
Mackintosh's architecture was accompanied by a flood of designs for
furniture, fittings and textiles. The chronology of Mackintosh's work in
these areas has been authoritatively established by Roger Billcliffe. The
work on the tea-rooms involved regular reworkings and alterations, and can
be thought of, more or less, as a 'rolling' commission. It is hard to date
the designs of some of the details in Mackintosh's buildings because,
in reality, alterations occurred in the course of construction. The paintings
fall into two discernible periods – the years of The Four (1893–1906), and
1923–7; but it seems likely that Mackintosh was always doing some
painting. The botanical illustrations associated with visits to Holy
Island, Walberswick; Portugal and elsewhere prior to 1914 may have been
intended by Mackintosh to form a book.

1864   Margaret Macdonald born near Wolverhampton in England.

1868   Charles Rennie Mackintosh born in Glasgow, Scotland.

1884   As Chas. R. McIntosh he enrols, aged sixteen, in the Glasgow
School of Art to take the Painting and Drawing Courses. First
apprenticeship with John Hutchison.

1885   Francis Newbery becomes director of the Glasgow School of Art.

1886   Mackintosh begins a course in 'Elementary Architecture'.

1888   Wins the Bronze Medal at the South Kensington National
Competition, the first of a series of such awards.

1889   Joins the firm of Honeyman & Keppie; friendship with Herbert
MacNair. Receives the Queen's Prize for his design for a
Presbyterian Church.

1890   Designs his first complete building – a pair of semi-detached houses
for his uncle. Silver medal for design of a public hall. Awarded
the Alexander Thomson Travelling Scholarship.

1891   Wins the Gold Medal for the design of a Chapter House. Gives
lectures to the Glasgow Architectural Association on 'Scotch
Baronial Architecture'. Undertakes an extensive Scholarship tour
of Italy, making many drawings.
The Macdonald sisters enrol at the Glasgow School of Art.

1892   Publication of W. R. Lethaby's *Architecture, Mysticism and Myth*.
Interior designs made for the Glasgow Art Club, under Keppie's

direction, and several other projects.
Meets the Macdonald sisters.

1893 Works on design of *The Glasgow Herald* building (completed in 1895 by Honeyman & Keppie). Quotes extensively from Lethaby in lectures.
Designs for a railway terminus published in *The British Architect*.
First publication of *The Magazine*, edited by Agnes Raeburn for students at the Glasgow School of Art.
Designs his first furniture, for the painter David Gauld.

1894 Works on designs for Queen Margaret's Medical College (completed in 1896 by Honeyman & Keppie) with considerable responsibility for the final building; drawing published in 1896. Works on several interiors for Honeyman & Keppie.
Drawing tour in south-west England. Many paintings and decorative designs. He and Herbert MacNair exhibit designs and craft-work together with Margaret and Frances Macdonald; they become known as 'The Four', and, with others, form the nucleus of a developing 'Glasgow Style'. Several pieces of furniture and other designs commissioned by the firm of Guthrie & Wells.

1895 Part-responsibility for the Martyr's Public School (completed in 1896 by Honeyman & Keppie).
Francis Newbery draws up the brief for the new Glasgow School of Art.
Drawing tour in south-west England. Works on the Buchanan Street Tea Rooms with George Walton.

1896 Begins work on drawings for the new Glasgow School of Art, encouraged by Francis Newbery. Proposal accepted. Also designs a church hall.
The Four show work at the Arts and Crafts Exhibition in London which is attacked in *The Magazine of Art*.

1897 Work starts on the Glasgow School of Art. Designs Queen's Cross Church. With George Walton, designs the interiors of the Argyle Street Tea Rooms for Miss Cranston.
Work of The Four praised in *The Studio*.

1898 Work completed on the first stage of the Glasgow School of Art.
Designs several buildings for the forthcoming Glasgow International Exhibition.
Work of The Four praised in *Dekorative Kunst*.
First foreign commission – a dining room for H. Bruckmann in Munich.

1899 The new Glasgow School of Art opens. Designs Windyhill for William Davidson (completed 1901).
Frances Macdonald and Herbert MacNair marry.

1900 At work on several projects, notably *The Daily Record* building (completed in 1901), as well as a number of interior designs and renovations, notably the Ingram Street Tea Rooms.
Marries Margaret Macdonald, and with her exhibits at the eighth Vienna Secession Exhibition. Triumphant reception in Vienna.
With Margaret, renovates apartments at 120 Mains Street (the typical 'white interior').

1901 Designs 'A House for a Lover of Art' (published 1902), with participation by Margaret Macdonald. Great professional acclaim in Germany and Austria.
Designs stands for the Glasgow International Exhibition, where the firm of Wylie & Lochead give much of their space to the Glasgow Style.
E. A. Taylor, John Ednie and others working for Wylie & Lochead. More work on the Ingram Street Tea Rooms. Drawing holiday on Holy Island.

1902 Designs Hill House, Helensburgh, for William Blackie (completed in 1904).
Designs a music salon for Fritz Wärndorfer, with contributions from Margaret Macdonald, who provides the cover for the May edition of *Deutsche Kunst und Dekoration*.
Major exhibition of The Glasgow Style at the Turin International Exhibition; some of the exhibited work is later seen in Budapest and Moscow.

1903 Designs Scotland Street School (completed in 1906). Begins remodelling Hous'hill for J. Cochrane. The Willow Tea Rooms begun.
Submits designs in the Liverpool Cathedral Competition.
Designs a small shop and house in Comrie (completed in 1905).

1904 Conversion of 78 Southpark Avenue for himself and Margaret.
Interior of Holy Trinity Church, Bridge of Allan.
Becomes a partner in the firm of Honeyman, Keppie & Mackintosh.
Publication over two years of *Das englische Haus* by Hermann Muthesius.

1905 Busy completing many projects. Work exhibited in Berlin.

1906 Further work on the Argyle Street Tea Rooms. Interior work on Abbey Close Church, Paisley.
Auchenibert House, Killearn (finally completed by another architect).
Mosside (house), Kilmalcolm.

1907 Further work on Ingram Street Tea Rooms. Designs second stage of the Glasgow School of Art: the Library (completed in 1909).
Departure of MacNair and Frances Macdonald to Liverpool and George Walton to London; the decline of the Glasgow Style begins.

1908 Interiors of the Lady Artists' Club.
Mosside, Kilmalcolm (second stage).
Visits Cintra, Portugal, where he makes botanical drawings.

1909 Further work on Hous'hill. Drawing and painting in the south of England.

1910 No commissions. Spends some of his time drawing and painting in the south of England.

1911 Designs the White Cockade Tea Room and undertakes further work for the Ingram Street Tea Rooms. Otherwise, very little work forthcoming.

1913 Resigns from Honeyman, Keppie & Mackintosh and decides to leave Glasgow.

1914   Moves to the village of Walberswick in Suffolk, England. Makes many botanical drawings.

1915   Moves to Chelsea, London.

1916   Renovation of 78 Derngate, Northampton, for W. Bassett-Lowke (completed in 1917).
Some small furniture and interior commissions. With Margaret, makes many textile designs around this time.

1917   Undertakes a further design for the Willow Tea Rooms.

1918   Produces designs for furniture for several clients.

1920   Designs for studios at Glebe Place, Chelsea, London. Much reduced version finally built. Several other studio houses and a theatre designed at this period but never built.

1921   Graphic design work.

1923   Settles at Port Vendres in the South of France and devotes himself to painting. Spends his summers in the Pyrenees. Despite exhibiting in Chicago and London, his work is unrewarded.

1924   Margaret Macdonald's last known design work.

1927   Returns to London for medical treatment.

1928   Dies in London.

1933   Margaret Macdonald dies in London.

List of Illustrations

Unless stated otherwise, photographs are by the author. All measurements are in centimetres, height before width.

1 Charles Rennie Mackintosh with Hamish R. Davidson, 1898. T. & R. Annan & Sons Ltd, Glasgow. Photograph.

2 Saloon in the SS *Arabia* (launched 1898) by Halsey Ricardo with William De Morgan. Photograph. National Maritime Museum, London.

3 Saloon in the *Fürst Bismarck* (launched 1905). Photograph. Strathclyde Regional Archives, Mitchell Library, Glasgow; reproduced by Courtesy of the Principal Archivist and Permission of the Keeper of the Records of Scotland.

4 Alexander Thomson, St Vincent Street Church, Glasgow (1859). Photograph.

5 Alexander Thomson. St Vincent Street Church, Glasgow (1859), detail showing west porch. Photograph.

6 Alexander Thomson. St Vincent Street Church, Glasgow (1859), detail showing capital in main hall. Photograph.

7 Alexander Thomson, St Vincent Street Church, Glasgow (1859), detail showing the end of a pew. Photograph.

8 Alexander Thomson, St Vincent Street Church, Glasgow (1859), detail showing a cast-iron pillar and seating. Photograph.

9 William Leiper, J. S. Templeton's carpet factory, Glasgow (1889). Photograph.

10 James Salmon jnr, 'The Hat-rack', 142 St Vincent Street, Glasgow (1899). Photograph.

11 James Salmon jnr, Lion Chambers, Hope Street, Glasgow (1906). Photograph.

12 James Honeyman, The Ca' d'Oro, Gordon Street, Glasgow (1872). Photograph.

13 C. R. Mackintosh, The former *Daily Record* offices, Renfield Lane, Glasgow (1897). Photograph.

14,15,16 Plant diagrams from Christopher Dresser. *The Art of Decorative Design* (1862).

17 John Ruskin, *A Spray of Olive*, 1870, pencil and bodycolour, 34.6 × 26.5. Ashmolean Museum, Oxford.

18 C. R. Mackintosh, *St Cuthbert's Church, Holy Island*, June 1901, pencil and watercolour, 20.3 × 26.0. Hunterian Art Gallery, University of Glasgow, Mackintosh Collection.

19 C. R. Mackintosh, *St Cuthbert's Church, Holy Island*, July 1901, pencil and watercolour, 20.3 × 26.0. Hunterian Art Gallery, University of Glasgow, Mackintosh Collection.

20 Edward Hornel and George Henry, *The Druids Bringing Home the Mistletoe*, 1890, oil on canvas, 152 × 152. Glasgow Art Gallery and Museum.

21 C. R. Mackintosh, *Sea Pinks, Holy Island*, 1901, pencil and wash, 25.8 × 20.2. Hunterian Art Gallery, University of Glasgow, Mackintosh Collection.

22 C. R. Mackintosh, *The Tree of Influence*, 1895, pencil and watercolour, 31.8 × 23.2. Glasgow School of Art.

23 C. R. Mackintosh, *The Tree of Personal Effort, The Sun of Indifference*, 1895, pencil and watercolour, 21.1 × 17.4. Glasgow School of Art.
24 Author's tracing from Mackintosh's *The Tree of Influence*.
25 Author's tracing from Mackintosh's *The Tree of Influence*.
26 Author's tracing from Mackintosh's *The Tree of Personal Effort*.
27 C. R. Mackintosh, *A Hawk*, 1896, pencil drawing. Hunterian Art Gallery, University of Glasgow, Mackintosh Collection.
28 Detail of a bedroom cupboard designed by C. R. Mackintosh in 1901. Hunterian Art Gallery, University of Glasgow, Mackintosh Collection. Photograph.
29 Detail of a living-room cupboard designed by C. R. Mackintosh in 1901. Hunterian Art Gallery, University of Glasgow, Mackintosh Collection. Photograph.
30,31,32 Author's tracings of roses by various Glasgow Style artists.
33 Author's comparative sketches showing five designs of roof-trusses by C. R. Mackintosh.
34 Author's sketches showing the plan and elevation of a domino table designed by C. R. Mackintosh, *c.* 1897.
35 C. R. Mackintosh, South façade of the Glasgow School of Art (1907–9). Photograph.
36 Author's sketch-plan of C. R. Mackintosh's School of Art (1907–9).
37 C. R. Mackintosh, Glasgow School of Art (1897–8), West façade. Photo.
38 Emblem on the title-page of Walter Crane's *The Basis of Design* (1898).
39 C. R. Mackintosh, Glasgow School of Art (1896–8), detail showing bay window on east façade. Photograph.
40 C. R. Mackintosh, Queen's Cross Church, Glasgow (1898–9), detail showing a capital supporting double beams. Photograph.
41 C. R. Mackintosh, Glasgow School of Art (1907), detail showing main entrance. Photograph.
42 C. R. Mackintosh, Glasgow School of Art (1907), detail showing stepped mouldings above main entrance. Photograph.
43 C. R. Mackintosh, *The Daily Record* offices, Renfield Lane, Glasgow (1901), detail showing entrance. Photograph.
44 Author's cross-section sketch showing roof-truss timbers and pegged joints as designed by C. R. Mackintosh for the Martyr's Public School, Glasgow (1895–6).
45 C. R. Mackintosh, Martyr's Public School, Glasgow (1895–6), detail showing timber brackets in the rafters. Photograph.
46 C. R. Mackintosh, Martyr's Public School, Glasgow (1895–6), detail showing stairwell and timbering above. Photograph.
47 C. R. Mackintosh, Martyr's Public School, Glasgow (1895–6), detail showing 'queen-posts' above the stairwell. Photograph.
48 C. R. Mackintosh, Martyr's Public School, Glasgow (1895–6), view from the north-east. Photograph.
49 C. R. Mackintosh, Martyr's Public School, Glasgow (1895–6), detail showing concrete brackets beneath a flight of stairs. Photograph.
50 C. R. Mackintosh, Mahogony Table, 1910. Hunterian Art Gallery, University of Glasgow, Mackintosh Collection. Photograph.
51 J. Paterson, drawing of a table in Hill House, Helensburgh, designed by C. R. Mackintosh in 1902.
52 C. R. Mackintosh, Glasgow School of Art (1907–9), the Library interior. Photograph.
53 Ernest Gimson, Bedales School, Hampshire (1919–21), the Library interior. Photograph by permission of Bedales School.
54 C. R. Mackintosh, Queen's Cross Church, Glasgow (1898–9), detail showing newel-post and plate at the head of a flight of stairs. Photograph.

55 C. R. Mackintosh, Queen's Cross Church, Glasgow (1898–9), close-up detail showing newel-post and plate. Photograph.

56 C. R. Mackintosh, Queen's Cross Church, Glasgow (1898–9), detail showing pillar and beam. Photograph.

57 C. R. Mackintosh, Glasgow School of Art (1896–8), detail showing stair-head iron grille. Photograph.

58 C. R. Mackintosh, Queen's Cross Church, Glasgow (1898–9), detail showing decorative wrought-ironwork. Photograph.

59 C. R. Mackintosh, Scotland Street School, Glasgow (1904–6), detail showing bolted steel joists. Photograph.

60 Margaret MacDonald, *The Heart of the Rose*, 1902, painted gesso panel, 969 × 940. Glasgow School of Art.

61 C. R. Mackintosh, mirror, 1901. Hunterian Art Gallery, University of Glasgow, Mackintosh Collection. Photograph.

62 Detail of the foot of a bed designed by C. R. Mackintosh in 1901. Hunterian Art Gallery, University of Glasgow, Mackintosh Collection. Photograph.

63 Detail of a cupboard designed by C. R. Mackintosh in 1901. Hunterian Art Gallery. Photograph.

64 C. R. Mackintosh, small table, 1901. Hunterian Art Gallery, University of Glasgow, Mackintosh Collection. Photograph.

65 C. R. Mackintosh, Hill House, Helensburgh (1902–3), hallway. Photograph.

66 C. R. Mackintosh, Hill House, Helensburgh (1902–3), detail showing stencilled design in the porch. Photograph.

67 C. R. Mackintosh, Hill House, Helensburgh (1902–3), wrought-iron gate. Photograph.

68 Detail of a bed at Hill House, Helensburgh, designed by C. R. Mackintosh in 1902. Photograph.

69 C. R. Mackintosh, Hill House, Helensburgh (1902–3), detail in living-room. Photograph.

70 C. R. Mackintosh, Hill House, Helensburgh (1902–3), detail showing light-fitting in the hallway. Photograph.

71 C. R. Mackintosh, Hill House, Helensburgh (1902–3), stairwell. Photograph.

72 C. R. Mackintosh, Scotland Street School, Glasgow (1904–6), detail showing Thistle-cum-Tree of Life motif on the south façade. Photograph.

73 C. R. Mackintosh, Scotland Street School, Glasgow (1904–6), detail showing decoration on the north façade. Photograph.